SONGS FOR THE PEOPLE

Art Solomon

SONGS FOR THE PEOPLE:

TEACHINGS ON THE NATURAL WAY

POEMS AND ESSAYS OF

ARTHUR SOLOMON

edited by

MICHAEL POSLUNS

NC Press Limited

Toronto 1990

Cover Art: Gerry Ginsberg
Design: Cathleen Kneen

Canadian Cataloguing in Publication Data

Main entry under title:

Songs for the People

ISBN 1-55021-058-0

I. Posluns, Michael, 1941-   II. Title.

PS8587.056S66 1990   C897   C90-093144-2
PR9199.3.S65S66 1990

We would like to thank the Ontario Arts Council and the Canada
Council for their assistance in the production of this book.

Thanks also to the Department of the Secretary of State,
Heritage Cultures and Languages Program.

New Canada Publications, a division of NC Press Limited,
Box 452, Station A, Toronto, Ontario, Canada, M5W 1H8.

Distributed in the United States of America by Seven Hills
Books Distributors, 49 Central Ave., Cincinnati, Ohio 45202.

Printed and bound in Canada

Acknowledgments

Many people need to be thanked for their part in the creation of this book. First, of course, is my wife Eva whose many sacrifices, voluntary and involuntary, have been behind all my work.

I want to thank Dr. Phyllis Fischer, whose strong support played an important role in making the book possible. And Ed Newbery, whose gathering of my notes and jottings was as essential to the creation of this book as my own writing.

I also want to thank Giselle Demontigny for her encouragement, Menno Wiebe of the Mennonite Central Committee Canada, Anne Fitterer and Michael Fay for their help. Finally, I thank my publisher, Cathleen Kneen, for her dedicated work in getting this book to print, all the people at NC Press who worked so hard on it, and Michael Posluns, for his persistence, enthusiasm, and careful editorial efforts.

Table of Contents

On Naming the Whole: A Note from the Editors

"My perception of God is that He embodies the ecstasy,
The totality, and the completeness
Of the sacred principles of male and female
But I address Him as Grandfather."

This is a book of meditations, spiritual reflections and prayers. Working with Art to assemble this selection of his writings over four decades we expressed interest in his use of Grandfather as his most preferred name for God. He told us that in the Nishnawbe language there are no pronouns. For us, this singular fact illustrated the extent to which the gender debate about the names of God reflects our own language and the cultural values and biases embedded in it.

Art says that, for him, God, the Creator is the totality of All, including male and female; but that when he prays it is as one of "His" creatures. Elsewhere he also speaks with reverence of the "Creation" and the "Earth Mother".

Our European-based culture automatically interprets this duality as a power relationship. Indeed, it is our notion of a male, active, powerful God who acts upon and has power *over* the female, passive, powerless Creation which has been the model upon which we have based our relationship to the Earth. In all his teaching it is precisely this attitude of domination which Art Solomon most condemns.

Art's understanding of the relationship between Creator and Creation is very different. It is one of harmony, mutuality and wholeness; and his teaching reflects that perspective. The movement for inclusive language which makes clear that God is neither male nor female – and that humanity is both – is a crucial part of the struggle for justice and equality between men and women. The teachings in this book, however, do not arise out of that cultural context.

Those of us for whom it is important to name the whole with justice and fairness will be strengthened when we hear these songs, not from our own cultural assumptions but with an openness to the Native way.

A Very Few Words and Their Meanings

Manitou: Perhaps the Nishnawbe word best known by English speaking people, *manitou* is most frequently translated as Spirit, Creator or God.

Kitche: Great. Hence, *Kitche Manitou*, Great Spirit.

Megwetch: Literally, "Thank you", *megwetch* is used both as an acknowledgement of a favourable act by another person and as a way of closing a prayer. It is this latter use which occurs frequently throughout this book of meditations.

Meewe: Literally, "enough", *meewe* is also used, on occasion, as a way to end a prayer.

Michael Posluns
Cathleen Kneen

Introduction

If this is poetry,
It is given and dedicated to the Native
Sisterhood in the prison for women
At Kingston, Ontario,
To the women's side of our Indian nations
And to all true women.

From your brother and Ojibway warrior
Ke She Ya Na Kwan
Who will never give up
Till hell has frozen over

In love
And dedication
And in solidarity
We must walk in beauty and with power.

CHAPTER ONE

The Singer and the Songs

Art Solomon, Kesheyanakwan, is a paradoxical personality. He has become a speaker for the traditions of the Native people and a voice for the justice for which they call out. Art's message is a spiritual and a social message grounded equally in a love for his own traditions and a recognition that the message of those traditions is meant to be shared with people of good will from every corner of the earth. If Art's fervour for those traditions has been reinforced by being cut off from his own people at an early age, his capacity for learning may also have been protected by being cut off from formal schooling not very much later.

Much of what Art has shared here was written in the still, small hours between days of meeting, counseling and teaching and doing the crafts which have been so central to his own message. Indeed, writing is one of the great paradoxes of Art's teaching. It has become a way of ensuring that the oral tradition from which he has learned throughout his life will be passed on to those who share his concern for the well being of the Creation.

Sharing a Native view with the world has led Art to follow a sometimes tortuous and difficult path which has often taken him away from the very people who have most inspired him – his vigorous mother and his strong and gentle wife, Eva. Art has had to make his own way and to become his own person in order to grasp the message he was meant to carry.

Art Solomon was born in Killarney, Ontario, a small, isolated lumbering and fishing village in 1913. He came of age and went out into the world in time to face the depression and the war years. When Art left Killarney to find work building roads, mining and carpentering, he was equipped with an elementary school education, a childhood training that had made him, as he says himself, "something of a loner" and a deep and abiding spiritual devotion that would change direction with experience.

The songs presented here reflect the spiritual progress of a single man and the seeds he sowed in that progress. The selection makes a particular emphasis on the movements he helped to inspire, and the social and spiritual issues those movements addressed. Another paradox is the frequency with which the movements inspired by Art's vision have blossomed into large and complex organizations: the Northern Ontario Craft Programme, the American Indian Movement, the Canadian Alliance in Solidarity with Native Peoples, the Native Studies Department at the University of Sudbury, the University Prisons Programme and the World Council on Religion and Peace.

In recent years, the paradoxes of Art's complex spiritual sojourn have been formalized as he has been honoured with the degrees of Doctor of Divinity by Queen's University in Kingston, and Doctor of Civil Law at Laurentian University in Sudbury, as well as the Ontario Bicentennial Medal.

Art has travelled widely in the last quarter century. His concerns have taken him throughout Canada, to Holland, Switzerland, South America, Mauritius, China and Australia. He has contributed his insights to several Christian churches, to Project Ploughshares, Amnesty International and the National Film Board of Canada, among others. In the last 30 years, Art has rarely received a salary but has laboured incessantly both for his own people and for world peace.

Art's songs are the teachings of a Native man whose spirit is fed by faith and by family. In 1938, he married Eva Pelletier. For most of their married life Art and Eva lived in Garson, near the city of Sudbury, Ontario. There, on rocky and, at that time, sulphur-blighted land, he created a renowned garden and a fine grove of trees. Visiting Art and Eva meant coming up over a knoll to find their oasis of greenery in the midst of a synthetic but barren desert. In 1980, Art and Eva acquired a long-deserted farm at Hartley Bay on the French River where Art and his sons rebuilt the old house and surrounded it with lawns and gardens. Art and Eva have ten children, each one a unique and distinct example of their parents' teachings. Like his teachings, they have made homes each in a different place, from Nova Scotia to British Columbia. Art guides and holds his large and scattered family by his own sincerity and sacrifice.

These songs are a blend of prayers to the Grandfather and Grandmother and teachings to his children. They are intended to warm, to cheer and to strengthen the people. Many were circulated in photocopy or mimeograph when they were freshly written. This selection places Art's various teachings in a context which we hope will give both permanence and honour to his life's work.

Art Solomon dedicates his life to his own people while he shares his Songs with all who value the re-birth of his people and the cycles of the Creation. He prays with the pipe and the prayer-book. He prays in the sweat lodge, the church and the prison cell. His prayers are to the "Grandfather and Grandmother" of all beings.

– m.p.

A SONG FOR THE PEOPLE

Grandfather, Great Spirit
  I give you thanks
  That we can sit here
  In this circle of Life,
  We send you our prayers
  And the very best thoughts

Grandmother Great Spirit
  As we raise this sacred pipe
  To give thanks to you
  And to all of your Creation,
  We give thanks
  To the spirit helpers
  Who came and sat among us.

Grandfather, Most sacred one,
  These are the prayers
  That we send to you
  As we sit here together and pray

Grandmother your children are crying.
Grandfather your children are dying.
  The hands of greed
  And the hands of lust for power
  Have been laid on them
  And all around is death and desolation
  The gifts you made, *for all your children*
  Stolen,
  And laid to waste
  In a monstrous desecration.

Grandmother Great Spirit,
  As we sit here and pray together
  We send you this prayer of affirmation –
  We your children whom you created in your likeness and image –
  We will reach out,
  And we will dry our tears
  And heal the hurts of each other.
  Our sisters and brothers are hurting bad,
  And our children, they see no future.

We know Grandfather, that you gave us a sacred power,
    But it seems like we didn't know its purpose
    So now we've learned as we sat together,
    The name of that power is Love,
    Invincible, irresistible, overwhelming power,
    This power you gave us we are going to use,
    We'll dry the tears of those who cry
    And heal the hurts of them that are hurting.

Yes Grandmother,
    We'll give you our hands
    And our hearts and minds and bodies
    We dedicate our lives to affirmation.
    We will not wait nor hesitate,
    And as we walk on this sacred earth
    We will learn together to celebrate
    The ways of peace, and harmony, and tranquillity,
    That come,
    From diminishing that negative, evil power within us
    And in the world around us
    Thank you Grandfather for this prayer.

HOW THIS PRAYER CAME TO BE

We had prayed the night before
With the Sacred Pipe.
In a circle,
Men and women together,
Next morning about four-thirty a.m.
I found myself wide awake and wondered why
I was so clear-minded after
Just coming out of a very deep sleep,
These thoughts, these words,
Were running around like butterflies in my head.

They wanted to be seen,
   They wanted to be heard,
      They wanted to be written,
         They wanted to become the reality for many people
            And they clearly followed from the Sacred Pipe
               The evening of the same night that they were written,
                  Before sun-up.

It is so clear that the "unseen ones",
The spirit helpers, want to work with us
And through us,
If we can only learn to stand aside and let it happen.
We need courage, and humility,
And an abiding faith in the God of all Creation,
Who not only made us, but very intimately keeps us going
Minute by minute throughout the years,
Who wants us to be His/Her helpers to accomplish the Creator's work.

GRANDFATHER, GREAT SPIRIT

Grandfather, Great Spirit,
  We are living in very troubled times.
  We see that everything is getting out of balance
  in this world.

  We see that our Mother Earth is very sick,
  We see that the water is too dirty to drink,
  We see that the fish life is poisoned
  and our people are dying from it,
  We see that the air is poisoned too and
  sometimes not fit to breathe.

  We know that you gave the air and the water
  a way to renew themselves so that your
  Creation could continue on this earth.

  We are sad to see that some of your children
  have gone that other way and they
  have chosen to destroy and misuse these gifts
  that you gave us.

  We know that You are the One who gave us life
  and that You made a place and food and medicine
  enough for all your children on this earth.
  We know that You made an equal inheritance
  for each of your children.

Grandmother, we are sad that some of our brothers
  have stolen our inheritance from us and that
  it has been that way for a long time now.

Grandfather, we see that You have given us a short
  time to accomplish our personal purification
  and to get ready for what is to come.

Grandmother, we the Native people of this land
  are crying for Justice and there is none.
  Those brothers that we ask, they give us lies
  and treachery instead.
  We know that nothing is hidden from your sight
  and that you are watching always.

We know that soon You will destroy evil
on this earth and restore truth.
Some of us, your children, are waiting and
preparing for that time.

Grandfather, *we ask for guidance and help* to find our way
back to the true way of living on this earth and
we need your help.

Grandmother, Great Spirit,
We thank You that You gave us life
and that You keep it going for us each day.

We thank You for our Mother Earth and that she is
still following your original instructions and that
she is still providing us food and medicine.

We thank You for our elder brother the Sun
that he is still doing the work that You gave him.
And we thank our Grandmother Moon that she is still
following your original instructions for her.

At last, we call on you, the spirits of the four directions
to help us because we understand that now we must claim our
inheritance. We must renew our ways of thinking and doing.
We must restore our humanity and go back to the true ways of
living.
We need your help and guidance because we know there are
only two roads to walk on and there is a great confusion
                    around us.

Meegwetch

VISION FOR MY PEOPLE

Grandfather, Great Spirit,
  Today I sat for a short while in the thundering silence of your solitude.
  And as I sat there I saw with my limited vision,
  The power and the sacredness and the beauty of your Creation.

                I give thanks for this new day.
                   Kitchi meegwetch!

This morning that strong warrior, our elder brother Sun
  Came up over the mountain, and he looked into my eyes, and he said,
  The time for sleep is over now. You must get to work.
I have brought a new day and a new chance, maybe a new way
  To see things. You must get up and do your part
  To make this a new world.

                I give thanks for this new day.
                   Kitchi meegwetch!

I looked and I saw a vision of how it was
  When I was still a little boy.
  The birds were singing their songs and building their nests
  In the way they were taught so long ago.
  The animals and the fishes and the plants and the sky world,
  They went about their work in the way they too were told so long ago.

                I give thanks for this new day.
                   Kitchi meegwetch!

I looked again and I saw how it was supposed to be,
  I listened and I heard it said that all things in your Creation
  Had been created, male and female.
  And of every kind, the fishes and the birds and the ones that walk
  and crawl
  And the ones that grow with the roots in the ground,
  Each had been given its original instructions.

                I give thanks for this new day.
                   Kitchi meegwetch!

All had been told that they were to grow to their greatest beauty
   And reproduce themselves
   And return again to the earth mother.
   In that way your Creation would be on-going, forever fresh and new,
   Forever power, and beauty, and sacredness.

I give thanks for this new day.
Kitchi meegwetch!

Then I looked at the vision of how it is and I saw this:
I saw might and devastation.
I saw prisons and vengeance.
I saw a vision of the greatest desecration in the history of man.
I saw leaders who are fools but who believed they were gods in
   their own right.
I saw those who were leading everything, even our earth mother,
   Into a final and total annihilation, without reprieve.
And I saw that you will not let it be that way,
                  Grandfather.

I give thanks for this new day.
Kitchi meegwetch!

I looked beyond the monstrous stupidity of these leaders
   And I saw hope.
For you had raised up good people who saw the final death.
And they said, "No! you cannot go that way!"
For we have reached out our hearts and our minds and our hands
   Across the continents and the oceans of the world.
And we will surround you and circumscribe you
   With an unbroken and unbreakable ring of prayer and hope
   For the continuation of our children and our future.
That is how it has to be.

I give thanks for this new day.
Kitchi meegwetch!

Grandfather, have pity on us
   And stop this evil power that grinds all in its mill of death
   Until nothing is left but nothingness.
   Grandfather, have pity on your children.

I looked again and saw the Indian Nations of this sacred Turtle Island,
  The ones you put here first and showed them their sacred way.
They too were despised and desecrated by those so blind and greedy.
But the sands of time run through the glass
And this time of times is nearly over.
The longest and the darkest and the coldest hour of the night
  Is the one just before the new day returns.
Now is the time of hope.
Now is the time to rise up.
Now we must take into our hands the power of self-determination.
We must stand up in our places in the sun.

> I give thanks for this new day.
> *Kitchi meegwetch!*

But I looked again
  And I saw there, alone in desolation,
    A woman, reviled and ravished and destitute,
      Her birthright stolen.
The teachings of her grandmothers had been replaced
  By thoughts that don't belong.
Yet she is the mother of our children.
Without her there is no future.

But wait, my brothers, let us take a closer look.
There stands our mothers and our grandmothers.
She is our wives and sisters.
Without her we cannot go
For that is how it was made to be,
That time so long ago.

> I give thanks for this new day.
> *Kitchi meegwetch!*

That woman is the mother of our nations,
  She is the centre of the circle of life,
  Fashioned by The Great Mystery
  And given as a gift to the male side of the human family.

> I give thanks for this new day.
> *Kitchi meegwetch!*

That woman, so troubled and so deeply hurt
  In the prisons of stone and steel,
    That woman imprisoned in the confines of her soul and mind,
      We must help her. For without her we cannot go.

My brothers and sisters, this too the vision gave:
  Those prisons of soul and mind are fashioned
  By cutting off the true knowledge, from The Great Mystery,
  And replacing it with mistaken ways of seeing
  And understanding that don't belong.
There, my people, is where we start.
We must turn back to the wheel of life again
  And help it to renew.

            I give thanks for this new day.
            Kitchi meegwetch!

We must turn back again and make our women strong.
Our women must search in their hearts and minds
  And in the understanding of their sisters
  For the meaning of woman.
  Then they must also search in the mind of God.
  And when they have finished there
  They must go back to us who are men
  For we too have our understanding of woman
  And without us they cannot go.
That is how it is supposed to be.
Thank you Grandfather
  For the power, and the beauty, and the sacredness of your Creation.

            I give thanks for this new day.
            Kitchi meegwetch!

THE TIME THAT IT IS

There is a time coming very soon, which is called by the Hopis,
the Great Purification;
when everything that is evil and obscene in the Creator's sight
will be wiped away from off the face of our Mother Earth.
When everything is made clean,
the Great Spirit power will start life anew on our Mother Earth again.
He will use people living now as the new human life to start over.
He will clean the water and the air
and all living things.
The time of the Great Purification has been spoken of in many ways.
It is also called the Apocalypse and the Revelation.
It is true that how you live your life is your business
and that's the way it should always be.
But the Great Spirit power who created all things –
the earth and the air and the water, the
fire, the food and the medicine and all that walk on the earth
or fly in the air or swim in the water –
He is still looking after all things.
He sees that nearly all His children are gone to a bad way –
the black and the yellow and the white and the red children
that He made. Nearly all are doing an evil way
so that there is no more peace and harmony
among any of His children or anywhere on the earth.
So He will come soon to destroy all that is evil,
and people will be destroyed as they have been many times before
on this earth.
But each time the Creator has saved some of His people,
"those who lived in a true way",
like seed to start a new planting.
This short time that we have left is for us to think
about the true ways and to ask ourselves in our hearts
if we want to turn to that true way.
We say there are two roads to walk on
and nobody can walk on those two roads at the same time
because they are far apart.
One is the road of destruction
and those who walk on that road are destroyers.
They destroy everything, they dig the gold

and the diamonds. They destroy the air and they poison the water,
and all living things are contaminated and hurt by their work.
They call that *progress*.
They work for money and power – power over people.
There are many Indian people following and benefitting
from the way of the great technology,
but how they live is their business.
There is another road.
It used to be called "the Good Red Road"
when our grandfathers and grandmothers talked about it.
The Good Red Road is the way of peace and harmony with the universe,
with the Creator.
We cannot be in harmony with the Creator and be out of harmony
with our Mother Earth or any of the life on it
including our brothers and sisters.
It is the way of peace and harmony;
it is the way of discipline;
it is the *Great Medicine Way*,
the true way of living and we can walk only on one road.
We have only a short time left to choose
and only the Creator knows how much time we have left.
Our Grandmother Moon is still following her original instructions
and our Elder Brother Sun is still doing his work
as he was instructed.
Our Mother Earth is still providing food and shelter and medicine for us.
Grandfather, Grandmother, Great Spirit, we, your red children
are in great sorrow and confusion.
Give us strength and give us guidance.
There is a great evil power that is devouring and destroying us.
Have pity on us because we are weak and we cannot see clearly.
Grandfather, Grandmother, show us the true way.

Meegwetch

Killarney is located on the tip of a peninsula at the mouth of the French River on the mainland of Georgian Bay across from Manitoulin Island, the largest freshwater island in the world. The fur traders had used Killarney when they travelled down the French River from Lake Nipigon to Georgian Bay and Lake Huron to avoid the Iroquois tolls on the Ottawa. Killarney was first settled by Europeans as a fishing village. During the latter part of the nineteenth century, lumber camps moved into the area, bringing further development to Killarney.

In the early decades of this century, Killarney was a village of 500 souls where the priest gave his sermons alternating between French and English while speaking with absolute authority. By 1913, Killarney was already predominantly English speaking. Killarney would remain a place of 500 people to the present day. It would lose its fishing economy only when the rivers and lakes were too polluted and the fish could no longer be safely eaten.

The Ojibway name of Killarney means "passing through place". Ojibway people drifted into Killarney from the north shore of Manitoulin Island and further west. Some had intermarried with French, Irish and Scottish settlers. This was the time when Indian people could not leave their reserve without permission of the government agent. Reserves were run under a federal Indian Act that said that "an Indian" was someone other than "a person". Church and state had combined to create a policy of assimilation. Killarney was a place where some Indian families came in the hope that, in return for the sacrifice of their traditional ways and the loss of their Indianness, they might gain a new way of life.

Art's family was among the third of the village that were Ojbiway. His father's family – like many of the Ojibway families in Killarney – had come from the north shore of Manitoulin Island. Art's mother had come up from Peterborough in southern Ontario. While she would remain an inspiration to Art throughout his life, she was an outsider who never found acceptance in the eyes of the extended family into which she had married. Art's father was a trapper, fisherman and lumberman who was rarely home and died when Art was fifteen.

Art learned to be a loner growing up at the family home on an island off the Killarney shore. He lived there until he left home to go to the residential school at Spanish, a town too far distant from Killarney for students to go home at Christmas or Easter. Art came home a second time, after a period working on the building of Highway 17, the road that would become the Trans Canada Highway. When the depression settled in, and his mother had re-married, he lived with an aunt and uncle who had a large but little used maple bush well away from the beaten track. Art spent several spring times alone at a sugar camp, tapping 500 trees for their sugar.

Art's spiritual home coming began many years later. After several years as an activist with the Mine, Mill and Smelters' Union, he was thrown back on his own resources when he was stricken with Bright's disease. A lesser man might have withdrawn from the world in the face of a crippling disease which left him with a very short life expectancy. Art chose a different path. He went out into the world carrying a message of hope to his own people on a very pragmatic level.

During the 50's, when the renaissance of traditional Indian communities was first beginning to take form, Art played a founding role in a number of Native organizations, most notably the Union of Ontario Indians. During the same period, he made a number of trips to Akwesasne, to help people there with his carpentry tools during the fall of the year. Akwesasne, a Mohawk community straddling the St. Lawrence River near Cornwall, Ontario and Massena, New York, had maintained its traditional Long House ways in the face of sustained adversity. It provided Art, as it has so many others, with a model of self sufficiency that is as instructive as it is illuminating.

The Long House taught Art that "every people has an original instruction" and that "the way to come under the Tree of Peace is to go back to your own roots." This lesson gradually coalesced for Art with a realization that, in order to be responsible for his own life he could no longer accept the paternalistic manner and teaching of the priest in Sudbury.

Pushed by one teaching and pulled by another, Art slowly found his way to the Midewin way, the traditional teachings, of his own Nishnawbe people. Over the next four decades, these teachings, and the experience of going back to his own roots, became the basis of the message that Art continues to bring to all the world.

– m.p.

YOU ARE AN INDIAN

March, 1985

You are an Indian
  And you are lost
    You don't know who you are
    Because you don't know where you have come from
    And if you don't know where you have come from
Then you can't know where you are going.

If you don't know who you are
  Or where you are going
    Then you are a nothing
    A zero;
    But in your heart,
    In the deepest part of your soul,
    You know that somehow
    That's not really so.

You somehow sense that you are somebody
  Very special;
    And you are absolutely right.
    But you've never been able to prove it
    To anyone,
    Not even to yourself.
And if you can't do that
  Then you must conclude
    That you really are a nothing, a zero,
    Like they are telling you.

You are an Indian
  You are a child of God
        Did no one ever tell you?
And whatever God makes is very special;
  He does not waste time making garbage.

You were not made by a man or a woman,
  You only came through them;
    They did not create the design, or the pattern
    They only followed the design of the master
    Because only God has the secrets of life.

Yes, you are very special
  Because you are a spirit being
    And only the God of Creation
    Can create a spirit.

But how do you liberate yourself
  From the trap you are in?
What is the key?
Well, I'll tell you a secret
  And this is how it goes:

A long time ago a man was lost at sea
  He landed on the beautiful shore
    Of this sacred Turtle Island,
    But he said it was "India".
Then others followed after
  And they had no eyes, and no ears
    So those were the teachers we followed,
    The ones who could not see and hear.
They said you have to count money,
  You must not waste your time
    Searching the ways of beauty,
    Just be like us and it'll be OK.

You must cut down the forests
  Kill the birds and the fish
    And the things that crawl, walk and run
    Because beauty is money and the things it will buy.
So we tried to be like them
  And forgot who we were
    And our purpose on earth;
    We followed blind leaders
    To the mess we are in.

We know how we got here
  And we know our way out;
    The roses don't say to the violets
    You must be like us,
    Because the roses are roses and the violets,
    they follow the way that's for them.

You are an Indian
  You belong to this land
    And a way was once given
    For "*Nishnawbe*" to follow.
But you can not find it
  By following blind leaders,
    You must look for the guides
    Who know their own way
    On this sacred land
    The *Nishnawbe* way.

And you, the non-status *Nishnawbe* child,
  You don't belong
    Anywhere.
Not in the Indian world
    Nor in the white one too;
    Because your skin is too brown,
    Your eyes are the wrong colour,
    Too many things wrong, you don't fit in nowhere.
So what's to be done?

Well, it's said
  There's no racism
    In the spirit world.
But what's to be done *Nishnawbe* child
  Here in this world?

Well, I have to say this:
  Every child of God needs to be loved
    And accepted,
    And nourished,
    And affirmed,
    And just as every flower needs sunshine
    So you have a need to be loved.

Those who reject you and put you down
  Because of who you are,
  Are rejecting the God who made you.
They are distorted, deformed,
  And in great danger
    Of losing
    Their humanity.

So *Nishnawbe* non-status child,
   You are like a flower in the garden of God.
You have a right to be.
And you belong;
   You are a child of God.
And being an Indian
   Is not only a matter of birth,
     It is also
     a
     State
     of
     Mind.

THE WOMAN'S PART

The woman's part in the Long House Confederacy
encompassed all of life, political, economic, social,
from birth to death, and growing food
and governing the people.
    In their tradition the line of descent
was through the women.
    It was the women primarily who chose
the chiefs or had them removed from office
if they did not serve the people.
    It was that way because from birth
to adulthood no one could know
more intimately what kind of person she was,
what qualities of heart and mind.
    But the men also had their part
in the choice because they saw and
understood as men.

    In the Ojibway tradition the line of descent
was through the men
but the women owned the food and the shelter
and all but the personal possessions of her man
and in all of the nations and tribes
it was known and understood
that the woman was "the centre of everything."
    The children represented the future
but the women were the present and the future
because without them there could be no
future for the nations; the cycles of life
could have no continuity;
the Creator's plan for human beings
would end.

    In each family the woman
was "the centre of the wheel of life".

    The women "were of the earth".
they were connected to the Earth Mother
and to the grandmother moon
whose work was to govern when all things
were to be born
plants, animals, humans.

Fertility was her working element.
Hence "the woman's cycle" or her "moon".
The power of birth was given to the women.
It was given by the Creator
and it is an immutable law.
It was given as a sacred work
and because it is a sacred work
then a sacred way was given to the women.
The woman stands between man and God.
She takes from both and she gives back to both.

This is the place made for her
by the Creator.
It is a place of highest honour
and the reason why men should honour women.
But equally, women must honour men
if not, then everything is out of balance
and we can have nothing but chaos and pain.
These are the first elements that must be put back
together or nothing – but nothing –
can come right again.

The woman is the first teacher.
Her teaching begins when the child is in
the womb and the only begins to diminish
as the father and grandparents and others become the
additional teachers.

The woman is the foundation on which
nations are built.
She is the heart of her nation.
If that heart is weak, the people are weak.
If her heart is strong and her mind is clear,
then the nation is strong and knows its purpose.
The woman is the centre of everything.

The Cheyenne people have a saying that,
no matter how strong our warriors
or how good their weapons,
if our women's hearts are on the ground
then it is finished.

It is there at that point where
the line of life was broken,
the instructions for the purpose and the meaning
of life were cut off,
and the little girls were no longer taught
by their mothers about the meaning
of a woman;
What God had in mind when She created women.
And it is that search that women must
begin and we must help them to get it
back together.
That is the absolute "first step".
The answers are in the spiritual
because it is a spiritual question.

WHAT IS A MAN?

My daughter, you asked me to define for you
what is a man?
I know you have thought a long time about that question
just as both of us in our own way and in our secret selves
have tried to understand for ourselves what is a woman?

Well, in my limited understanding, I will try to share with you
what the years have taught me.

What I write for you is written in humility
and with the understanding
that after all these years of suffering and striving
I still know very little of anything.

But as one human person reaching out
and trying to help another human being to a better understanding
of the purposes of life, and how we should see ourselves,
I offer these thoughts to you.

A man is a mature male person
whose maturity is not to be measured in years
but in his sexual maturity and in his ability
to cope with the requirements of life.

He has the ability to cherish and protect
and care for his female partner and for whatever children
the Creator may choose to bless them with. But wait,
this is too simple a definition of what a man is.
Because if we hope to get some true understanding
we will have to go back and consider his parents and we need to think too
about his grandparents;
we need to think about the environment
that all of them grew up in
because we are conditioned by our environment
just as surely as the plants and the trees are.

If we had the mind of the Creator we could go back to the
beginning, but then if we had the mind of the Creator
we would have no need.
We would already know.

Since we are human beings with our limited understanding
we have to be content with whatever definitions we may arrive at
for our understanding of what is man or woman,
or what is the purpose of life.
It seems impossible to my mind
to describe what is a man or a woman or what is life
without also saying something about human sexuality
because for us who where born of a father and a mother
human sexuality was the first principle involved.
That is what made it possible for us to be born.

The environment that the man grew up in as a boy
is not the environment of air and water and trees and land
not those things.
it was the human environment,
created by warm and loving and understanding male and female people,
people who accepted their sexuality as natural gifts
given to them by the Creator
for the enhancement and enrichment of their lives, gifts that were
good and wholesome and even sacred.
Throughout their lives they kept a spiritual contact
with their Creator and they understood and accepted
that they were of the Creation
just as the plants and the rocks and the water and the air
and the sun and the moon and clouds,
and though they may never have put it in words
they understood that the laws or instructions were the same
for them as it was for the plants and animals.

Those instructions were put into the subconscious or the real
or *soul person*
I say the subconscious or *soul person* to differentiate from
the intellectual or *front person*.
Those instructions were:
(1) the determination to survive individually and
(2) the need to mate sexually.
In order to survive as a people, those instructions
were given by the Creator in order that His work of Creation
may continue.

So the man that we are looking at
grew up into his manhood in that wholesome and good environment
and that environment was the same for his mother and father
and for his grandmothers and grandfathers and his aunts and uncles
because they were a part of his life too
and they shared love and understanding with him when he needed it.

There was one tremendous contrast
between the life ways of those people and the people
that we live with now.
Those people had their humanity intact.
They had their spirituality.
They were a part of the throbbing rhythm of the universe
and they knew it
because they could feel it in their bodies.
They did not have needs based on greed.
Their lives were based on the rhythm and the fruits of the seasons.
They did not have incredible expectations
of the bounty of the Earth Mother or of each other.

So I think it is here
where we can begin to get some understanding of life
when we contrast the way of harmony
with the life ways of the people who live here now.

Many of the people who live now have incredible
and impossible expectations
of life and of each other.
Many were cheated of their inheritance
along with their parents before them.
There is almost no one who is not tied,
hands and feet, soul and body, hope and expectations
to the rhythm and the requirements of the great industrial machines.

If they want to live and mate and eat and drink and enjoy life
they must do it according to the dictates of the machine
and he is an all powerful god, without heart or emotion
or feeling of any kind,
his master is a greed that devours everything within reach
including human beings
and his high priests are those faceless people who control
not only the most powerful countries of the world
but literally the destinies of all the people of the earth.

If any of us want to live through the time
of great purification that is coming
we have to think seriously about purifying our own ways of thinking
and looking to see how we can get ourselves back
into harmony with the creation again.
I think there is very little time.

May the Creator direct your ways till you come to walk on His road.

TO BE A FATHER

June, 1983

To be a father;
What does it mean?

To be a father is very simple.
Just find a female partner and mate sexually with her
And if everything is right,
The woman will have a baby
And you will be a father.

A new human being will have come from the spirit world
To live in this part of the Creation.

Then what?

Well, first of all, I think is is necessary for us
As men and women to look at the world
The way it is now,
And to look at the world the way it was,
And then to look at the world
The way it is supposed to be.

If we want guidance for us as men and as fathers
We won't find it by trying to fit into a system
Based on false values.
Rather we must look for guidance
In a system of values and principles
That are based on the power and the beauty
And the sacredness of the Creation.
In other words, we must search for an understanding of
The fundamental laws of the Creation.

If we do not soon learn to live by the laws of
The Creation,
We will be destroyed by its power.

If we want to learn how to live
By the power of the Creation,
And in harmony with it, then we have
To learn something about its fundamental principles.

Everything in the Creation is created
Male and Female.
Everything is based on that
Sacred principle, and from it flows
All life, to accomplish its destiny
As the Creator intended.

It was the Creator who invented the
Sacred Male and Female principle.
And from that follows the Life Force and the imperatives
Of all living things.
It is the Male and Female principle which guarantees
The ongoing Creation for everything that lives,
Whether it be plants, animals, fish, birds, air or water;
Everything.

We as Male people have been given the gift
To help with the Creator's work in His ongoing Creation.
The Female side of the human family have been given the other part
Of that gift.
We as Male or Female people are self-sterile;
We cannot reproduce ourselves without the other side.

And we are created as equals,
Not one to be subservient to the other.

A few years ago two men and a woman
Sat late into the night talking about life.
The woman only listened to what was being said.
Finally, at last, she spoke.
And this is what she said:
She said, This is how I understand about life.
She said, First the Creator made a man
And set him down on the earth.
Then He watched him and thought about him for a long time
And somehow there seemed to be something wrong. Something missing.

So He made a woman,
A female partner.
He gave the woman His choicest gifts
Of shape and form and mind and heart.
He gave her special qualities and abilities.
And He came to the man

And He said to him:
Here is a gift that I have made for you,
Someone to make you happy and to fill your life
And make it complete.
Here is a woman. She will be your partner.
You must cherish her and honour her.
She is my gift to you.

So what would it be like if men and women
Could see and understand in that way again?
Because that is how it was.

To me, the Creator, the Supreme God,
The Great Mystery, is both male and female,
And it is the complete unity of those sacred
Principles that makes heaven.

So what is the man's part once he has become a father?

Well it seems to me that if he is going to do that part
In a good way, he needs to recognize and accept
Some of the fundamental principles involved.
One of these principles is that
First of all the child is a spirit being
In human form. It is a child of God
With its own destiny to accomplish.

The second principle is that man was given only a very small part
In the conception and birth of a new human being
The major part was given to his female partner.
And it may be true, as I believe it is,
That the greatest ceremony that is possible
For human beings is the conception
And formation and birth of a human child.

And to do that, the woman receives both from God
And from man, in order to fulfill her purpose in life.

That is the work of woman.
And I believe that the woman's place is between
God and man.
Not because woman made that choice but because
The Great Mystery gave her that place
At the center of everything.

It seems to me that if we, as Native people,
Begin to see life in this way again,
Then our relationships might start to come
Back into balance again.
I think we have to make some choices and accept
The responsibility for those choices.

Some years ago we said
To this mad society:
"We are going back", and they said,
"You gotta be right off the wall.
You can't go back to bows and arrows
And tipis and no clothes on!"

We were hurt by that argument
Because we were not sure what it was
That we were going back to.
We knew it wasn't bows and arrows.

Finally it dawned on us that we were turning
Our backs on this insane technology
And going back to the ways that give
Purpose and meaning to our lives.
To the ways that the Creator had intended
For us to follow.

So guess who's laughing now?

CHAPTER THREE

In a Weary Land

Art Solomon is the quintessential craftsman. Art's childhood and adolescence had given him a knowledge and love of craft work to which he returned to gather strength when he was stricken with Bright's disease. As important as the specific knowledge of different crafts was the loving patience to work with natural materials to create a work of practical and enduring value. His songs begin in the work of his hands. His home and its surroundings are eloquent statements of his skill at accentuating the beauty of natural things.

Art has long seen the making and selling of beautiful crafts from natural materials as a way in which Native people could improve the quality of life in their communities. By the 1960's, Art had been independently fostering craft work among Native people for a number of years. He had witnessed the importance of crafts wherever native culture was undergoing a re-birth and been saddened by the economic pressure on crafts people to produce for a tourist market which lacked any sense either of the function or the art of traditional craft goods.

Art frequently gathered and supplied materials which he would offer to craft workers in return for goods they might later produce for which he would find a market when he travelled down south. There was, for example, an abundant supply of quills in the Killarney area, at that time, because the new road led to the death of large numbers of porcupines. Art gathered these quills to trade at Wikwimikong and elsewhere on Manitoulin Island. As important as the quills and other materials, he planted new ideas and revived traditional designs for making crafts from which people with no other likely source of cash might make a livelihood.

In 1964, Art travelled to New York City where he helped found the World Craft Council. The Council had been founded on the idea that bringing together the crafts people of the world was an important step in fostering peace. When he returned to Canada, he helped found the Canadian Craftmen's Association in 1965. Six months later Art was asked to be a director at large to encourage Native crafts.

During this same period, Art was engaged in the creation of the Indian Hall of Fame at the Canadian National Exhibition grounds in Toronto. Through this activity his work became known to a number of people close to the then federal Minister of Indian Affairs, Arthur Laing, who was eager to find projects for his Department's economic development branch.

Art's attention had, at that time, become fastened on the condition of Indian reserve communities in the far north of Ontario; communities such as Angling Lake, Webique, Bearskin Lake, Sachigo, and Kasabonika where the limitations of reserve life and the depletion of game had long been eroding the quality of life for the people. Art's own success with wood and leather and bone led him to believe that a way might be found to improve the economic lot of the people in the north through the skilled use of these available materials.

Despite his own reservations about working for the government, he was finally persuaded that he might put their resources to good use while also learning a great deal by spending time inside the heart of the beast. In 1966, the Minister offered Art a position with the Department of Indian Affairs and Northern Development to develop a crafts programme for northern Indian communities. Art was seconded to the Ontario regional office in Toronto, where the director simply said that northern Ontario was beyond his territorial responsibility. Nonetheless, the northern crafts programme got off the ground and was modestly successful for a year and a half. After several exploratory visits a Native Crafts Guild was set up to encourage the creation of such things as the people chose to make from materials at hand, and to market these things in the cities in the south.

Neither Art nor the others who offered their services properly understood the half-hearted nature of the commitment of the Department of Indian Affairs and Northern Development to an Indian Craft Programme until the government scheme began to unravel two years later.

Art's response to this betrayal of trust is expressed in his own preface to his paper on *Craft Development*.

– .m.p.

CRAFT DEVELOPMENT
HUMAN DEVELOPMENT
COMMUNITY DEVELOPMENT

August 6, 1969

This paper entitled "Craft Development" was written in desperation after seeing for myself during two years the utter impossibility of any hope for a realistic craft development opportunity within the bureaucratic confine of the Indian Affairs Branch, it was written at Kasabonika on May 29, 1969 under the most impossible conditions. I apologize for nothing, except that it could have been better written. I thought at first that the Indian Affairs Policy Statement in June 1969, had made it obsolete, but it has not. I find it absolutely incredible that such a policy could have been devised and vigorously promoted at the federal government level in Canada. Such treachery and denial of human justice in Hitler's Germany or Ian Smith's Rhodesia I could have understood, but not here in Canada in 1969.

Kasabonika, Ontario, May 29, 1969

The bare essentials of our proposals were to establish a limited company in which the craftsmen could have voting membership and they would in time control the entire operation by electing directors of their own choice. The marketing agency we proposed would have acquired the existing stock of the Indian Affairs Branch crafts centre in Ottawa as part of its starting inventory, we would have taken the whole business completely out of the hands of Indian Affairs. It was obviously this part which they could not accept.

This company would have been operated for the benefit of the craftworkers on a cash and carry basis, there would be no charity involved, because charity is not what the craftworkers are asking for, they only accept charity because *the total conditions* give them no other choice.

Such a company could hold the large amount of capital required and direct it in a profitable ways. I would have a capable board of directors serving without pay to guarantee an operation which is in the best interests of the craftworkers and capable of meeting needs of the market on realistic terms.

This company would be a marketing organization capable of buying those raw materials required by the craftworkers in large quantities at the lowest possible prices and re-selling them to the craftworkers *at cost.*

The essence of such a company is a pool into which the craftwork can flow at its own rate and from which the retailers can draw on as their needs dictate, something which can be consistently reliable as to quality and to some extent quantity. It would actively promote and market the sale of Indian crafts by a policy of going out and selling.

It would provide *buyers* who are in essence the key people. They control the quality because they would not buy below a certain standard. The buyers would organize the supply of raw materials and sell them to the craftworkers, they would be constantly in touch with the market by regular visits to the marketing people and when necessary by mail or telephone. In this way the craft workers are constantly in touch with their market and they can produce marketable products to the limit of their capability and desire, and be assured of a constant market and a steady income.

Our proposals were a detailed plan for immediate action *and we requested immediate action*, the proposals called "Canadian Crafts Limited" were delivered to the Indian Affairs Branch in June of 1966. It called for a year of testing in Ontario in order to better modify itself to the needs of the craftworkers, before gradually expanding in 8 years to cover all of Canada, because it was a *national plan* for craft development.

One of the reasons we pointed out for an early start was to take advantage of the centennial year Expo, in 1967.

In May of 1967 the bins and shelves of the Indian Affairs Branch crafts centre were completely empty except for a few bins of garbage souvenirs which were a disgrace to behold.

The cries were loud and long that year across the land because of this missed opportunity, strangers from other lands were most bitter in their disappointment.

There was no problem to buy handcrafts from other countries at Expo, because their variety seemed endless and inexhaustible, but where were the Indian crafts? Well this I know, that much of the best was reserved for visiting dignitaries who came to Ottawa from other lands and it was pitifully little.

When our proposals were delivered to the Indian Affairs Branch Regional Office in Toronto, the officials after studying them called in Mr. Bruce Pearson, the man who co-ordinated and directed the work. They were highly indignant. They gave every reason why our proposal wouldn't work. The only possible answer to them was, when you guys get off your fat behinds and get out there and study this situation with open and sincere minds, then come and tell me what its all about, until then hold your mouths. That was the end of our 40,000 dollar proposal right there.

I have met some good people in Indian Affairs but they were in positions where they could do very little of real value, they always gave me their good wishes. I fed my dog on good wishes once when I was a boy; and he died.

In order for a "craft development" to happen two basic essentials are required:

1.   A marketing organization free to operate in the market as a business and capable of handling at least some of the existing potential now and with the ability, in resources and facilities, to expand to meet the potential production of those craftsmen who want to use it when they see its usefulness to them.

2.   An immediate need is a buyer or buyers who will go to the craftworkers and pay cash at reasonable prices for their good quality work. The buyer would need to be a person who can appreciate crafts and craftsmen, understand his own work and at the same time be able to deal face to face and pay for articles according to their quality and value, not according to sentiment. A person who can refuse to buy from a craftsman without losing his friendship.

3.   Of equal importance is to have a creative person who can set up workshops in communities for the purpose of putting on exhibitions of crafts, for teaching, and above all to stimulate creativity and originate new ideas which can become marketable products. Such a person would require a lot of mobility because he must constantly gather a lot of information as well as share a lot.

Why is a "Craft Development" needed?

1.   First of all the Indian craftsmen are among the most deprived human beings in Canada. Secondly, where the need is greatest, in the economic sense, is in the more remote parts of Ontario, here the need is desperate and immediate, and also the capability and the desire of the people is greatest.

For the past year I have had a program of craft development underway in 2 northern communities, Kasabonika and Webequie in Northern Ontario, and even though it was tremendously hampered, simply because it had any number of bureaucratic hindrances and requirements, it proved beyond any doubt that it was very valuable and absolutely essential from the point of view of the craftworkers.

It was a simple matter of giving the initiative into the hands of the craftsmen and insisting that it stay there, in other words I didn't "do for people" but with them. I constantly insisted that at any point if they were not satisfied they must cancel the whole thing. They often had some hard decisions to make.

They had to stop practically everything they were skilled at making because the crafts centre kept insisting, "I don't want moccasins, I don't want mukluks, I don't want beadwork" or any other things they were making, "I want something else", so we made abstract carvings which created an immediate demand which we have never been able to satisfy, as well as other new items.

2. A *craft development* means that hundreds of thousands of dollars a year would get into the hands of the Indian craftsmen *as earned money*. Its beneficial effects would be immediate to the whole economy.

3. The Community of Cape Dorset in the Arctic (total population 500) earned $167,000 last year from the skilled work of their minds and hands.

4. Indian people are entitled to an opportunity *on their terms* which befits their dignity as human beings, they are entitled to an investment in them as the original owners of this country who have been robbed of their land and even their identity and prevented from accomplishing their destiny.

5. Handcraftsmanship is the most primitive, the most modern, and the most excellent means of self expression available to man for those who make and for those who enjoy. "Crafts development" is perhaps the most significant part of human development. It is the most natural and least troublesome means of economic development for these people who have almost no other way to earn money.

Craft development is a very essential part of the development of most nations of the world and instead of diminishing now in this age of modern technology it is a need that is expanding. In a few short years it will become one of the vital life factors of our times unless we succeed in destroying ourselves first.

6. Last year, 1968, an estimated 40 million dollars worth of gifts and souvenirs were sold in Ontario, *80% of it imported.*

The shopkeepers and the buying public are constantly looking for good *dependable* supplies of Indian crafts of good quality, they would buy an unlimited quantity. Why aren't they getting them from the Indian craftworkers?

First of all the whole thing is such a chaotic mess that it almost defies description how Indian crafts get to the consumer was fairly well outlined in our proposals "Canadian Indian Crafts Limited" but it was only an outline. It would take thousands of dollars and a book to describe it and nothing would be gained. In fact the whole study and the money to do it would be more money and time wasted.

The shopkeepers ask, "Where can we buy good dependable supplies of Indian crafts *when we need them*", and the Indian craftsmen ask, "*Where can we sell?* Indian craft workers need to be sure of getting their money without being exploited to death".

It is useless to tell the craftworkers about markets and how and where to sell. I'll give you an example.

During this past winter I informed the craftworkers of retail shops and individuals which I had personally contacted and who wanted to buy from them. Almost without exception I took the work to my home in Garson and there packed them and shipped them at my own expense. At least 7 times out of 10 when I saw the craftworkers again, they'd say we did not get our money so I'd have to sit down and write letters time and again.

The shopkeepers (and individuals) order an article or articles and then when they receive them they are indifferent and even sometimes don't pay for what they have received. In one instance a shop in Ottawa had a shipment sent prepaid during the first week of April this year. It is now the middle of June and they are not even sure they will get their money. Their value on those goods was $351.75. More than two months have gone by since they sat down to produce those articles and they are not even sure they will get paid, but the craftworkers first have to pay cash for their working materials.

How long would you wait for your paycheque? Could you be constantly frustrated year in and year out and still be willing and happy to produce for a market that may be very large but from which you can almost never get any satisfaction? Would you still have initiative?

In another case one women sent a pair of home tanned moosehide bead embroidered mukluks to a woman who had ordered them. The value was $25.00 plus other articles to the value of $45.00. They were shipped during the middle of March when transportation is good. This is the middle of June but where is the money?

The same woman who produces only the very highest quality of work, sent a moosehide jacket with beautiful bead embroidery on it to a man in Toronto. The jacket was made in March and shipped prepaid the first week of April, again no money has been received. On *July 28th* the craftworker wrote me to say she still hadn't received her money. Yet the question is always raised, "Don't the craftworkers have any initiative?"

This is the normal experience of the craftworkers year after year, the only difference was that they had skilled and experienced help to ship their goods out in time and the results are no better.

One more example. One of the carvers and his wife from Kasabonika worked at the Canadian National Exhibition last summer to demonstrate their skills at the Indian Hall of Fame exhibit. One apparently very concerned person whom they knew before, offered his help *without cost* to sell their work for them after they left. They sold a fair amount to the Canadian Guild of Crafts in Toronto, who could not sell it all. They had also brought along some of the other peoples work from Kasibonika. In this case they either had to take the things back or trust someone to sell it for them. They left about $350.00 worth behind and never received a cent nor can they find any trace of the man. Will they ever get justice for this kind of thievery? *For them it will be impossible.*

Do you think that under such impossible circumstances that they should be left to help themselves as best they can? And that is not all the problems by any means. It costs anywhere from *10 to 15 cents a pound* to ship goods in or out and by aircraft is the only means for many communities.

It is a fact that much of their good design has been lost or bastardized or replaced with religious symbols and in a great majority of cases the craftsmen have been forced to produce souvenir junk to satisfy the meanest kinds of taste.

Imported Souvenirs

What we must do is to help the craftsmen to produce high quality hand-made things but of a quality and nature that will take the craftsmen out of the senseless competition with foreign machine made junk.

The good original Indian designs are timeless and excellent. It is a simple matter to develop a whole range of new products based on materials native to each locality. Diamond willow abstracts are just one example of using a native material which is not only plentiful throughout Canada but is a commercially useless scrub wood.

So there are *unlimited possibilities* for development in this area alone *but to explore them we must be free people*, free from bureaucratic hindrance and requirements and *with money enough to be able to work and plan one logical step after another* but always working hand in hand with the craftsmen, using their ingenuity and their initiative as the driving force. They are tremendous people if they just get half a chance on their own terms which means simply *within their frame of reference* and that is what every human being is entitled to as a natural right.

A Pool

What is required in essence is a marketing organization free of government control and bureaucratic meddling and which can buy in quantity and re-sell at cost those things which the craftworkers need such as thread, beads, cloth, tools, etc. This marketing organization is a pool, if you like, into which the craftwork can flow and from which the retailers can buy.

Bees do not gather honey in the winter. They gather it when the flowers are in bloom and store it for future use. There is absolutely nothing wrong with gathering crafts during the best production months and selling them when the retailers need them the most. It is the logical and sensible thing to do. We had proposed just such a plan as this. It is just as valid today as it was three years ago, *only more desperately needed.* Our proposals died aborning because the midwife was the gentle and loving Indian Affairs Branch.

It is not right to assume that all Indian people are good craftsmen or that all want to be but it is true that a very high proportion of them are or want to be craftworkers simply because of their desperate economic circumstances and because it is the most natural first step to a better way of life in which they are the people making the vital decisions. Furthermore, there are no people in Canada more adept at translating ideas into artifacts where the vital factors are ingenuity and natural skill acquired over centuries of necessity. The first requirement is not a matter of finding teachers and setting up classes but of presenting a realistic opportunity and then challenging the ingenuity and natural skill in order to develop new products. Requiring modifications in traditional products to suit today's market is no great challenge any more than the day to day problems that we constantly live with.

The idea that seems to prevail everywhere that Indian people can not establish and operate their own craft operations is mostly a myth propagated and maintained by Indian Affairs to keep themselves in jobs and security and to maintain the *traditions of empire* for which they are so noted and hated.

I do not believe that a craft development can be started in *any Indian community* in Ontario and hope for success in a reasonably short time. I know by experience that every Indian community is as different from the next as individuals are. The most vital factor which makes for quick success or dragged out indifference and possible multiple failures is the *social or cultural factor.* If an Indian community is situated close to or within a non-Indian community it is usually at some stage of cultural and social disintegration, sometimes close to total disintegration. In addition to the natural or unnatural destructive forces at work there are the distractions such as beverage rooms and television, so in a sense it would be something like beating a dead horse to try to start a "craft development" in such a community.

The most remote communities stand ready, willing and able to start at the word "go", but that word "go" must be something of substance. It has got to be people working with people free to develop as people must be.

If the craftworkers are to have a reasonable opportunity to sell their work in a market which is often a thousand miles from them, it is essential to consider the matter of subsidy. If you were a craftworker in far northern Ontario you would be more remote from Ottawa than Cape Dorset in the Arctic. To sell your work in Toronto about 1200 miles away, you would have to pack your craftwork, ship it by aircraft to the nearest railway station up to 250 miles away, with air freights costs up to 15 cents a pound, to two other carriers before it got to the railway and once it got to the railway it might eventually get to the customer in good order with the craftworker paying the cost of shipping.

What am I asking for?

I am asking for an investment in people. I am also saying that Government has no business doing for people what they can best do for themselves. In this case it means letting people run their own affairs, but Government does have an obligation to help poor and deprived people to help themselves.

If there is going to be a real development of Indian people which will enable them to take their rightful place in the affairs of Canada than it is imperative that the Indian Affairs Branch be entirely and completely demolished as soon as possible and only be re-constructed in consultation with the national and provincial Indian Brotherhoods and Metis society, and only serve those needs delegated to it from those consultations. The more I've seen of the Indian Affairs Branch and its methods and controls, the more certain I am of a sinister and deliberate plan to perpetuate itself all the way to eternity, even though it swears from time to time that its purpose is to work itself out of a job.

Native peoples in the United States have generally been exposed to the pressures of urbanization and industrialization for a much longer period, and often more intensely than in Canada. Indeed, historically, Canada frequently found itself in the position of being a prime beneficiary of United States Indian Policy without generally needing to face the messy business of open warfare.

In spite of the fact that the United States has more frequently entered into treaty with various Indian nations, and that these treaties have the force of law, there has evolved a tradition of Indian policy in which the treaties have been "more honoured in the breach than in the observance". Even the distinction between the United States and Canada, and the border separating them is, from a First Nations perspective, an artificial distinction made for the purpose of separating peoples. Across the continent – from the Micmac on the East coast, through the Long House people along the St. Lawrence, the Nishnawbe in the upper Great Lakes, the Blackfoot on the prairies and the Salish on the west coast – the boundary which, by treaty, was not meant to apply to the First Nations was run through the middle of their lands.

The formation of a militant spiritual response to the continuing oppression of Native peoples, in the 1960's and early 1970's, the *American Indian Movement,* was hardly restrained by a boundary separating brother from sister.

Art's own teachings and personal experience found a resonance in the American Indian Movement for which he had long been seeking. Art became deeply, and at times, dangerously, involved in its two-fold goal of protest and Native renewal. He welcomed such a movement with his own special intensity, opening his house to travellers from every corner of the continent, taking its message into the prisons, sharing in its various manifestations. Art found himself under frequent police surveillance both on the road and at home.

Art's writings during the A.I.M. days reflect his mood of confrontation and anger in meeting what he called "the genocide machine."

– m.p.

THE NATURE OF POWER

The nature of power is that it is given
  by God to God's children.
At the moment of conception.
There are four:
  the woman and the man
  And God and the new life.

To that new human being
  God gives that one his gifts
  and his destiny,
  and the power to accomplish that destiny.
It is that power
  of self determination
  that is stolen away
  by wrong teaching, by lies and myths
  and compulsory mis-education
  and one more child of God becomes
  a mis-fit in God's plan
  mentally, emotionally, psychologically
  and spiritually.

That's how it is in Indian land.

WARRIOR SOCIETY

The American Indian movement sees itself
  as a new Warrior Society for Indian people.
There are various concepts of a warrior society.
To White people, the warrior is the armed forces.
Its the guy who goes out there and fights and kills for his people;
  paid soldiers.
But Indian people have never had hired killers.
Warrior Society to them means the men and women of the nation
  who have dedicated themselves
    to give everything that they have to the people;
      A warrior should be the first one to go hungry
        and the last one to eat,
          He should be the first one to give away his moccasins
            and the last one to get new ones.
That type of feeling among Indian people is
  what a Warrior Society is all about.
He is ready to defend his family in time of war –
  to hold off any enemy – and be perfectly willing to sacrifice
    himself to the good of his nation and his people.
That's what a Warrior Society is to Indian people,
  and that's what we see ourselves as,
    what we idealistically try to be.
That's not saying that we are all completely selfless
  or any kind of saints, but we try,
    with the spiritual direction of our holy men,
      to get ourselves to the point where we don't have
        the avarice and greed that is so much a part of white society
          in this land.
We believe that the power of this universe is held
  within our peace pipe.
It is a pipe of peace, a pipe that at all costs tries
  to guide us in avoiding any deaths by our own hands,
    or any violence on the part of the American Indian Movement,
      and if anyone will check back into the history
        of the American Indian Movement,
          though we take a very strong stand for our people,
            we've never killed anyone.

We have never had violence
  unless violence was perpetrated against us.
The real violence in America is committed by the government
  against our people.
The real violence is the fact
  that on a reservation our women are taken and
    raped in the back seat of cars.
Our job is to regain our humanity and our spirituality
  as it once was,
    our job is to fight for freedom against oppression,
      our job is to fight for land to stand on;
        land, a part of our Mother Earth
          which will be our physical and spiritual power base;
          we are freedom fighters.

WHAT IS A.I.M.?

A.I.M. is the American Indian Movement; it is not to be confused with the United States of America where it was born out of the violence and the hatred of white American police and white American citizens.

A.I.M. was born out of the blood and the anguish and the despair of suffering Indian people who saw that either they must lie down and die under the heel of the oppressor or they must stand up and live.

A.I.M. is not an organization. It is a movement. As the spirit of God moves through the earth and over the earth, so does the American Indian Movement. If the spirit of God can be stopped from moving where it will, so can the American Indian Movement be stopped.

A.I.M. is a spiritual movement, its basic concept is based on the freedom of the human spirit, freedom which was created by God himself and not by the laws of man.

A.I.M. was born out of the violence of five hundred years of living with a civilization of vultures, a society of parasites, a society of hypocrites, a people who *talk and sing about love but practice hatred*.

A.I.M. is truth, it is the stark naked truth of young and old Native people who are willing to die for what they believe in, and what they believe in is the dignity and worth of all the living things that the Creator has made; they believe that one human life is worth more than all the money that can be piled together in one place on the earth.

A.I.M. was born out of the brutality of the enforcers.

A.I.M. was born out of the anguish and the despair and the blood of countless Native people, spilled in the name of a false God.

A.I.M. is truth and *our only weapon is truth*, truth and the sacred pipe, the sacred ceremonies brought to our old ones from the spirit world.

A.I.M. is Native people saying to a brutal society, "if you have nothing more sacred than money to live for, we DO."

A.I.M. is native people of North America determined to restore their humanity by returning to the old and sacred ways of their ancestors.

A.I.M. is a freedom movement. What we want is peace and good order on this earth, our Mother, so that our children will have the right to live as free children of the one true God the Father of all men and the Creator of the universe.

A.I.M. is a freedom movement but we know that freedom is not won with words. Freedom is won by people of action. Freedom can only be won at the price of pain and blood, there is no other way.

A.I.M. is Native people who see that there are only two roads to walk on this world, one is the road of peace and harmony with the universe of *life*, one is the road of power and greed, *materialism*, and *death*.

A.I.M. people have chosen the road of life, they know they have chosen the Creator's way, the one marked out for all the children of God from the beginning of time.

A.I.M. is Native people who have seen the *way of death* grow and expand and cover the earth with its evil ways, until everything is contaminated with its many poisonous ways of thinking and doing.

A.I.M. is Native people who see the great evil power turned against them in its final fury.

A.I.M. is Native people knowing that our grandfathers and grandmothers were the keepers of this land and remembering that it will be returned to the true people of the earth again when it has been purified.

A.I.M. is Native people preparing their hearts and their minds for the great purification that is soon to come now.

A.I.M. is the Native warrior society of today and it is said that their bond is the *bond* of the sacred drum, they vote with their bodies and not with their mouths, their business is freedom, whatever the cost, they fear not death but life which is a living death.

A.I.M. is Native people in America who see the laws of the land for the lies that they are, and they see the enforcers for the goons that they are, and they see that their business is death.

A.I.M. is young Native people who have been ripped off from their parents by the missionaries and the Children's Aid Societies, they see that life for them and their children is a diabolical joke that they have to live with, their lives are destroyed and their inheritance has been stolen, there's nothing left to lose.

They see that the strangers who come in violence must soon be *the victims of their own violent ways*. Those who sow the wind must reap the whirlwind. Those who come with the sword in one hand and the bible in the other hand. Those who stole their brother's land and their right to freedom with lying documents that they called treaties. Those who called their brothers savages and pagans and thought them less than human will soon have to reckon with the Father of all men. For all of Creation is sacred and all of Creation has one father and those who desecrate their Father's work will have to answer.

What will they say?

There is an old Micmac legend from long ago that says "Some day there will be a people come to this land, Turtle Island. They will have hair like fire, Norsemen, but they will not stay long, Then other people will come out of the sea; they will have white skins but they will have no eyes and no ears." A Micmac who is old now heard this legend from his father when he was a small boy. As he thought about it, he wondered, "My father must be crazy to say that because how could a people walk around with no eyes and no ears?" But as he grew up and became involved in the struggle for justice and dignity and human rights, he said, "Now I understand what my father tried to tell me long ago, 'They have no eyes and no ears,' because when I have tried to tell them: 'Do not destroy, do not harm the earth, don't make the water and the air filthy, do not multiply lies and untruth, do not be unjust toward your fellowman,' but no matter what I show them, they show me that they have no eyes and no ears, because they seem to do all manner of evil things as though they believe that there is no God that we will have to account to for our time on this earth."

ADDRESS TO CHRISTIAN CHURCHES, FROM THE NORTH AMERICAN INDIAN MOVEMENT IN CANADA, 1975

It's at this time that we address our words to you, the Christian Churches of Canada. We hope that you will hear what we have to say.

We see that you have dedicated 10 days of this year, 1975, for world development. We think that is a good thing since you are a part of the majority society that has so consistently ripped off everything from what you call the Third World.

We are very concerned that in this work of Ten Days for World Development you seem unable or don't want to see the massive injustice that is being done to us, the Native people of this land, and we want to advise you that it can't go on that way much longer. And we also want to remind you that the Man of Galilee once said, "Whatever you do to these my brothers, you do also to me."

We are sad and very angry that our people must die by eating poisoned fish so that you can have your kleenex and your paper napkins and your newspapers, whose work is to distort the truth so that your artificial world can keep going.

We are aware of the horrible and lingering deaths of those Japanese people who have also been poisoned by mercury. And we have not forgotten that atomic bombs were dropped on Hiroshima and Nagasaki. That was the "gourd of ashes" spoken of in the Hopi prophecy. That prophecy was known long before the white people came to America.

We recognize that the family of man was established on this earth by the great creative power of the Universe, and that we are a legitimate part of the family.

We recognize that when we were conceived in our mother's wombs, the Creator was there at the moment of conception.

He is the one who gave us life.

He is the one who fashioned the destiny of each new life.

He is the one who gave to each one his gifts and the power to accomplish his own destiny.

We are aware of how the power to accomplish our own destiny was stolen away from us by the lies and the laws and the treachery of the white race who came to this land, and we are bitterly aware of how they have disgraced us and especially our women, since they came to this land that was once clean and good to live on.

We would remind you not to be misled by talk about importing violence from the United States because it is not true: It is true that you who came from Europe long ago, you are the ones who came in violence and you have lived in violence ever since, even to this day. You cannot live that way much longer because our Earth Mother is repulsed by your violence and our prophecies tell us that the purification of this world will soon come.

It is you, the dominant society, who have sown the wind. We are well aware of the great damage and disruption you have caused in our villages by setting up your many churches and dividing us against one another with your different religions. We saw you literally fighting each other for our souls while you seemingly cared nothing for our living bodies. That has been the experience of our mothers and fathers, grandfathers and grandmothers and now ourselves.

We remember how you worked to destroy our spirituality and replace it with the hypocrisy of the majority society, and we see that some of the churches have redoubled their efforts to make us "be like them". But we will not worship material things and put them above human values. In that way we refuse "to be like you".

We are sad and we are angry when we look around at our Native brothers and sisters and we see them committing suicide because they have been robbed of their inheritance, and life is meaningless to them.

We are sad and angry when we see our brothers and sisters destroying themselves and their children with your alcohol and the dissipations that you invented.

We are sad and angry that you came to this land and you said in your arrogance "They are savages and they are pagans, we must Christianize them and make them civilized."

Do not tell us about Christ crucified on the cross because these many long years we have watched Him crucified in this land by your judges, by your laws, by your governments, by your police, and by you the churches.

We see the hypocrisy of your "Christian" ways, and the destruction that you have done among our people these past 400 years in the name of Christianity.

We *had* a way of peace and harmony with the Creation around us because we saw that it was the work of the Great Mystery, and in humility we thanked Him each day for all the gifts that He gave us and we trusted Him.

We did not have money that we could write on it, "IN GOD WE TRUST". We have inquired about the name of that God who seems able to make his subjects behave in strange ways and we have found that he has some strange names, *Avarice, Greed, Lust, Hatred* – those are some of his names.

At this point we propose the question of *genocide* to you, and we propose three modes of commission: *physical, biological,* and *cultural,* taken from considerations of the United Nations in some of their earlier debates on the crime of genocide. And we add to that a fourth mode, *spiritual.*

What follows here are some extracts from some of those debates:

1) The planned disintegration of the political, social and economic structure of a group or nation.

2) The systematic moral debasement of a group, people, or nation.

Genocide has two phases:

1) Destruction of the natural pattern of the oppressed group.

2) The imposition of the natural pattern of the oppressor by a synchronized attack on the life ways of the captive people.

Cultural genocide is effected by the destruction of the specific characteristics of a group; by forced transfer of children to another human group; forced and systematic exile of individuals representing the culture of a group; the prohibition of the use of religious or historical documents or monuments, or their diversion to alien uses.

A culture's destruction is a very serious matter because a healthy culture is all-encompassing of human lives. If a people lose their "prime symbol," that which gives their lives purpose and meaning, they quickly become disoriented and lose hope, and social disintegration follows.

It is this burden that we lay on your shoulders, *cultural and spiritual genocide,* which you practised on our parents and on our grandparents and on us.

We have cried for justice in this land but there is none.

How can outrageous injustices be done in front of your eyes like on Parliament Hill on September 30, 1974, and in your prisons and other places of torment, yet you do not lift a hand?

We do not hear your voices raised for justice.

We wonder about your Christianity because we are your brothers.

All we wanted was to be left alone in this land to follow in the sacred ways of our ancestors.

We do not come to you with our hats in our hands, humbly asking for favours.

We come to you in our own right as men of vision, as human beings, demanding that you act in a Christian, human way, on our behalf, as you are able and when opportunities arise, to intercede with governments and in favour of justice and truth in this land.

We give you this document today in the knowledge that never in this world or in the next you be able to say *WE DIDN'T KNOW.*

THERE IS NO MIDDLE GROUND

There are many people who have seen the way things are,
  And have asked almost in despair,
    But what can I do?
And the only answer has been,
  You have to do something about *You*.
Only you can decide whether you will be a part of
  This destruction or whether you will set your
    Heart and mind against it.
You may not be able to change where you work or how
  You earn your living,
    But you are totally responsible for the direction that
      You give your own life.

We are only visitors here in this part of Creation,
  We are guests of the one who owns this Creation.
We are always to keep in mind that we
  Can own nothing here, not even our own lives.
So the purpose of life then is
  Not to acquire possessions
    But to honour the Creator by how we live.

If we chose to be on the side of that great Positive Power
  We have no choice but to set our hearts and minds
    Against the destruction around us,
      But thought without action is useless.
We must be on one side or the other
  And how we will involve ourselves must be the free choice
    Of everyone.
If we choose to act, we must act intelligently
  And with common sense.
It means we will do everything in our power to understand
  The questions that we choose to involve ourselves with.

But whatever we are, we must be action people
  Even if the only action possible is to pray.

Power is given to each of us by the Creator.

They are on a journey, they have chosen their way.
They will restore their humanity.
They will take their place in the sun.
Will their path be a road of anger and bloodshed?
Or will it be a road they can walk on in honour and peace?

A new nation of people will be born again,
    the sacred colour of red will be restored
        and no power on earth can prevent it.

You, that other colour of man,
    can assist at the birth of this new nation,
        Will you?

We are ready but we have no land,
    we have no money and
        we have no place,
        we have nothing but the anger and
        the frustration of our young people.
We have our vision and we have our hopes.
    We have our understanding and
        we know the way and we want to
        teach our young people again before it is too late.

We have our plans but where are those who will help us?

Of the dominant society it has been said:

                They have no plan to prevent crisis.
                They have no plan to anticipate the crisis.
                They have no plan to alleviate the crisis.
                They have only a plan to suppress the crisis.

                They have no plan for opportunity.
                They have no plan for equality.
                They have no plan for justice.
                They have only a plan for repression.

We suggest that you people begin to talk with us
    because it is FIVE MINUTES TO MIDNIGHT.

THE WAY IT IS IN THE INDIAN WORLD NOW, DECEMBER 1974

A LONG TIME AGO a strange people came to this land. They were strange in so many ways and they are stranger still today.

They came and they planted crosses and the flags of strange kings in our Mother the Earth and they claimed ownership over Her and all that She provided for Her children.

We had understood for untold centuries that our Mother the Earth and all that was seen and unseen in our world and in the universe had been created by the Great Mystery and that He alone was the owner of all things and that we, His children, were given life by Him and that in our short time here on this world we are to give honour and thanksgiving to Him each day as we walked about on the earth.

We understood that to honour Him we had to regard his plants as sacred and He taught us which were to be used as medicine and which ones to use when we prayed to Him like the *sacred tobacco, the sweet grass, the cedar, and the sage.*

We saw that the animals had a life like our own and that their life was sacred and precious to them. We regarded them as our brothers and we knew that when we killed one of them for food we must give thanks to the Creator, to our Mother Earth, and to the Guardian Spirit of that animal, and so we tried to walk on this earth in a sacred way.

We observed the rhythms of all the Creation and we saw that everything in the universe – the sun, the moon and stars, the water and the wind, the night and the day, the summer and winter – each was doing its work according to its original instructions from the Creator. We patterned our lives and our work according to that sacred rhythm. We saw that the Creator had provided everything good for our needs and we trusted Him.

It was the Creator who gave us the sacred pipe to pray with, and He was the one who taught us the sacred purifying way of the sweat lodge. It was He who taught us the sacred songs so that we could grow abundant food in the desert. He heard us when we prayed in that way for rain. It was He who taught us about the four spirits who had a special work to do for us while they guarded the four quarters of the earth.

It was the Great Mystery who gave us our visitors and our medicine people, and He was the one who gave us our prophecies and our sacred ceremonies. Our prophecies told us about those strange people who would come to this land and the great troubles that we would have to live with. Our prophecies also told us about the Great Purification that is about to begin very soon now and how we must prepare ourselves for that time.

We were not perfect but we gave honour and thanks to our Mother Earth and to all things. We saw the great harmony of everything around us and we patterned our lives accordingly. We prayed and we trusted. We apologized to a tree before we took its life to support our own. We prayed before we pulled them out of the ground for our food or our medicine. We did not kill what we did not need. We believed that the life of each plant or animal was sacred and we offered the sacred tobacco to its spirit. We believed that in giving honour to all things that we were following in the way of the flowers and the plants who were giving the greatest honour to their maker by blossoming to their greatest perfection.

We were not perfect but we had no jails and we had no judges or lawyers and no policemen. We had no taxes and we had no wine and no beer and no whisky.

We had no money,

We had no old peoples' homes,

We had no children's aid society,

We had no crisis centers

We had no atomic bombs, no hydrogen bombs,

We had no warplanes

We had no warships

We had no standing armies.

We honoured our dead, we honoured our people and our children, and we honoured each other. We had self discipline and a code of moral conduct. We had a philosophy of life based on the Creator and harmony with all of His Creation including his spirit world, *And we had our humanity.*

We did not know about Christianity but we had our spiritual way that governed everything about our lives and we believed that God was our father. We did not know about scalping until the strangers came and taught it to us. They called us savages and pagans, but we always fed those who were hungry even our enemies.

There are two great powers in the universe. One is the Great Mystery that we call the Creator. We also call Him the First Worker. The other great power is the great Evil One and there is a great war between them which is very near to its climax now. That war can only end in one way. There is only one who can win and He is the Creator of the universe. His winning will be the time of the great purification when all that are working on the side of the great Evil spirit will be destroyed and all their works will be wiped away with them. Then the earth will be renewed, our Mother Earth will be like a young woman again. The water and the air will be clean. The animal life will return as it was. All the food will be clean again. That human life that the Creator has preserved from among those living now will be re-started in a pure way again with their instructions about how to live on this earth.

Those strange people that come to this land of North America and South America called us savages and said they were going to civilize us. They said they had a mandate to Christianize us too. In some cases, they gave us a choice: either join their religion or have our hands cut off or be killed outright. They must have been very dedicated Christians to put it that strong.

Christopher Columbus said that the Native People he met were clean, handsome, and gentle people and "they would make good slaves". He tricked some of the first ones to come aboard and did make them slaves when he got them back to Europe.

Sieur De La Salle said, in a petition to his king, in 1677 that "these countries will infallibly furnish, within a few years, a great many new subjects to the church and the king."

When these strangers who came were few and hungry our people welcomed them and fed them and gave them shelter. But in time the strangers grew many and with excessive greed and treachery they began to make what they called "treaties." No matter how much land they got they always wanted more, so that our brothers the Sioux People came to call them *"Wasichus"* which means, *those who take everything.*

And these *Wasichus* made laws and they made armies and they stole everything, with promises, "treaties", that they never intended to live up to. As one wise old chief said at the time,

"they, the White people, made a great many promises and they never kept but one, they promised to take our land and they did."

Once we were dispossessed they put us on *reservations* often at the point of a gun, and the laws were made to make sure that we remained a disinherited people. The courts and the armies and the police were sent to make sure that it stayed that way till this day, in 1974.

But it was not enough that we were put on reservations, often on the poorest land around. Our dead were dug up and put on display. We were ridiculed and humiliated in the most hateful ways. Our children were carted off from the love and the customs of their families, forbidden to speak their mother tongue under pain of cruel punishment.

The people who did this insisted that they were Christians and that we must become Christianized.

The whole story of the rape of the people and of a continent is written in books as it was once written in blood. It has got to be one of the most sordid accounts in the history of mankind. But in their haste and their greed and their arrogance the *Wasichus* forgot that *whatever you do to your brother you do also to God.* Now we are close to the time of accounting.

They forgot that when you foment hatred against your fellow man you also foment hatred against his Creator. They forgot or never knew that we had and still have, a philosophy based not on the acquisition of material things but on a harmony with the Creator and the rhythm of his Creation, that is how we fitted into the timelessness of the universe, time belonged to the great mystery and we did not have to concern ourselves except to be in tune with it.

But those strangers who came had strange ways, they made machines to measure time. They made machines to measure everything. Because they were takers, they took everything, from the earth and from the water and from each other.

"We who have been so artfully dispossessed and so oppressed for so long, we have watched the takers taking."

We have watched them making their artificial world and living in their critical ways. Some said, "God is dead." and "We only live once", "Sex has got to be free." We wonder about a people like that.

These *Wasichus*, we have watched them for hundreds of years now. They never stopped taking so we had to conclude that they have a philosophy based on material things: They measure; and, they make laws; and, they put fences around where no one can go; they put people in jail because they try to feed their hungry children.

They dig gold out of the ground and they bury it back in the ground. They put armies around to guard it. If somebody tries to take some they kill him. We see always that money is more important than human beings. But these people they mark on their money "IN GOD WE TRUST." Yet they act so strangely toward other human beings. They must have a strange God.

We see that these strange people have almost entirely lost the humanity they must have once had and we see that many Native people have adopted many of their ways, so that they have become as deceptive as the ones they copied from. Now at this time it's almost impossible to find any one who still speaks true words and tries to live in a true way.

So we have turned back to look at the old prophecies that our old people told us about long ago and we are determined to go back to the true human values and the true ways of living on this earth because we must purify ourselves to be ready for the time of great purification.

We see that some of our brothers, of other races, are already doing that too. We are beginning to insist on our rights as children of the Creator. We are beginning to restore our humanity, regardless of the increasing oppression by the majority society.

They want more electricity, they want more coal, they want more oil, they want more land, they want more water, they want more slaves. We the Native people of the land, we stand in their way. We stand as a reproach before their faces, not only for their past misdeeds but for the even more monstrous misdeeds that they plan to carry out now.

And you of the majority society, should know it is your governments, it is your laws, it is your police, it is your guns that are pointed at our heads. So that your industries can have more consumers to consume more.

It's a money society but the money is dying like our old ones said it would. What will you do then? Our old ones also said that when the time comes our young people would wear braids and go back to the old ways again and that time is now, and we are hated because of it.

When you go to your churches on December 25 and you pray for peace, you should remember that war is not made in the capital cities of the world, *It is made in the hearts of men* – by men and women who choose to work on the side of evil power but still call themselves Christians, men and women who pray to the real God but give their hearts to another.

In 1969, the University of Sudbury, through its Religious Studies Department, began a course in Native Studies. The purpose was to explore the values of the natural religion of the First Peoples of this continent. Ed Newbery, the founding chair of the Department, credits Art as an inspiration behind the creation of the Department, a new and radical idea in its day. Art's interest soon deepened the concerns of the course from the theoretical to the human and social levels and also enriched its spiritual qualities.

The course developed into a programme of courses and then to a Native Studies Department of the University. In recent years, this Department has contributed to the formation of a new Native Social Work Programme in the Department of Social Work of Laurentian University.

The Native Studies Department of the University of Sudbury has attracted a considerable number of Native students to its classroom courses. Even more have enrolled in its extension and correspondence courses and in its summer school programmes. The strengthened Native organizations have often utilized and also often contributed to the resources of the Department.

Perhaps most important has been the development of the prison programme, a systematic programme to provide Native inmates of both federal and provincial institutions with the opportunity to study traditional Native culture and values. The prison program developed when Ed Newbery persuaded the Donner Foundation to fund the cost of Art Solomon's travels to bring Native spiritual services to inmates in prisons throughout Ontario. Art had already begun to do as much travel as he could manage from his own pocket. This support allowed him to provide spiritual counsel to Native inmates on a regular rather than an ad hoc basis. It also allowed the development of an extension programme designed specifically for the needs and situation of Native inmates. The prison programme, in turn, led to the establishment of the Newbery Halfway House in Sudbury, for men and women on probational release from prison. Another development has been the Burwash Native people's project.

In all this activity and growth, Art was an active and guiding presence providing both teachings and leadership essential to the development of each new programme or project.

– m.p.

THE RENAISSANCE

The nature of the spiritual and cultural rebirth
   of Native people is not easy to describe.
But I will use this way that seems the easiest.

The nature of the rebirth is like this,
   When the sun comes up in the morning it shines
      on the higher ground first, it warms up the ground,
      and the air, and the plants, and the people,
      They see it and feel it and understand it.

But on the lower ground it comes later.
And in the deep shade the perception
   comes very slowly and very poorly.

The ones on the higher ground
   are the leaders, the elders and the spiritual people.
They are the ones who see and feel and understand
   the nature of "The Bundle" that has been left behind.
It is they who understand the nature and the meaning
   and the power of those sacred ways.
That "Bundle" contains the original instruction
   and the sacred teachings that were given
      to our people so that they could conduct themselves
      in honour and reverence toward the Creation.

The nature of the renaissance is like the sun coming up
   in the morning.
And there is no man who has the power to stand there
   and say to the sun, "Don't come up just yet
      because I am not ready."

The rebirth is an imperative which has its source
   and power and direction from the great mystery, the
      Creator,
      who created the four colours of man,
      four sacred colours.

God created all humans equal
　　and it was never in God's plan that one colour
　　　　of man should oppress another,
　　　　　　whether by economic slavery or whatever
　　　　　　　　form of domination
　　　　　　　　　　The imperative which drives us will overcome
　　　　　　　　　　all obstacles no matter how formidable,
　　　　　　　　　　　　because there is no power that can stand
　　　　　　　　　　　　in the way of the Supreme Power.

EDUCATION

The traditional way of education
    was by example and experience
        and by storytelling.

The first principle involved was total respect
    and acceptance of the one to be taught.
And that learning was a continuous process
    from birth to death.
        It was a total continuity without interruption.
Its nature was like a fountain
    that gives many colours and flavours of water
        and that whoever chose could drink as much or as little
            as they wanted to and whenever they wished.
The teaching strictly adhered
    to the sacredness of life whether of human
        or animals or plants.

But in the course of history there came
    a disruption.
And then education became "compulsory miseducation"
    for another purpose, and the circle
        of life was broken
            and the continuity ended.

It is that continuity which is now taken
    up again in the spiritual rebirth
        of the people.

PHILOSOPHY

There are two different philosophies which
    have always been the fundamental difference
        between the people of the land,
            and the strangers who came here from Europe.
One is a philosophy based on the concept
    of materialism: ownership of land and possession
        of things.
It is a false concept because only God
    can *own* what He created.
And we are only visitors here in this part
    of His Creation,
    We are His "guests",
    We have come from the spirit world
    and we must return to the spirit world
    again and there we must make an accounting
    for the time and the opportunities and the gifts
    that were given to us to accomplish
    our individual destinies.

The philosophy of the original people
    was based on the timelessness
        and the harmony and the power of the Creation
            and humanity's place and purpose in it.
And because of the fundamental difference
    we could not, and we never can
        "be like them".
God never intended for roses to become daisies.
And so it must ever be.
And because we will never be
    "like them" they have despised and rejected us.

OUR WOMEN PEOPLE

These things that I write will always be incomplete because they come from the understanding of only one man. But it comes from the agony of watching many of our young women literally wallowing in mud for a long time.

It is written not to criticize but to help our women to become strong and true people again and I apologize to you our women for not understanding more or expressing myself better. Because I understand something of your power and your dignity and the work that was given to you by the Creator.

I am not saying foolish words when I say, it is something like standing in front of God and telling Him, "Hey, you've got dirty feet".

So it is in that way that I want to express these thoughts to you in the hope that it will begin to make you strong again.

In the past few years many of our young AIM women have come to me to ask the agonized question, "How can I put my life back together in a true way again?" Why do our young men show no respect for us anymore? Why are we down so far in the scale of human values? Why are things so bad that life is no longer worth living?

Why? Why? Why?

It is not only our AIM women who ask for answers to these terrible riddles of life but many young women of the majority society too, and some of them I care about very much. So it is these kinds of questions that I want to address myself to. Perhaps I have some advantage because I speak from the perspective of a man's understanding, which is sort of looking from the outside in whereas you must look from the inside out. And that is precisely why we need other's help in understanding ourselves.

I think that I also have the advantage of years because I have thought about the question of women and what they were doing (in the context of the majority society) during the past 45 years at least. Surely no one can consider a question for that long without learning something about it.

A Woman's Power

I hope you will not misunderstand me or take offence when I say that a woman's power is primarily sexual power. That is so because that is the way that the Creator made it.

But a woman's power is not only that. It is also a spiritual power, an intellectual power, a moral power too and it is many undefinable things more besides. It is undefinable because every woman is a unique individual with her own special gifts of heart and mind and emotions, and it is further undefinable because every woman is a mystery even to herself because she is an essential part of the Great Mystery who created her for His own sacred purpose, and that purpose was so that his Creation could keep on going.

It is perhaps at this point that we should consider "What is a woman?" More than a year ago I wrote a description of what a woman is and I want to include it here in the hope that it will be as useful to you as it has been to others.

What is a Woman?

It is my belief that if our women do not come to understand what a woman is then I don't think that they can ever find answers to the exceedingly grievous questions that trouble them. And if our women are sick and weak then their man and children will be sick and weak, and very troubled too.

It is not by chance that in all civilizations girls are often called by the names of flowers or linked to flowers and I believe there are two reasons why that is so. One is because of the grace and beauty of form that they grow into as they come to maturity and the other reason is that they are so nearly identical to the flowers in helping to reproduce humankind.

The role of women, or as I prefer to call it, the work of the women in this Creation must not be defined by men alone as it has been for centuries past. And it can not be done by women alone. It can only realistically be done by women who call their men to sit and counsel with them after they have carefully tried to understand it among themselves first.

This is why in the past I have asked our women to consider the idea of forming a women's council so that they would make their own council fire and there think about life and its meanings for us as a people. Because its only when we begin to put these things together in a right way again that life will begin to assume its true meaning for us once more.

A woman is a mature female person who is aware of the physical gifts that were given to her by the Creator. She has some understanding of what they are to be used for and she has some idea of the special part that was given to her in the continuity of Creation. She is aware that no new human life can be born on this planet except through a woman. She is aware of the great power that was given to her because of these special gifts that are hers. She is aware that to the children and the old people and to the men she is like the centre of the universe and that without her everything would come apart and disappear. She is the heartbeat of our mother earth, and without a heartbeat there is no life. The woman is the foundation of her nation from which her people derive most of their spiritual power.

A woman is a part of the Creator who made her and because that is so she is part of the Eternal Mystery that the Creator is, a Mystery which no human mind can begin to understand.

The mystery of a woman is part of her sacredness because it is part of the mystery of the universe.

The sacredness of a woman is in her ability to receive the seed of her man and in the co-operation with the Creator to fashion a new human life, for the faces of the ones still coming towards us can not come to life except through a woman.

The sacredness of a woman is also in the many gifts of heart and mind and soul that were given to her by the Creator.

Our women were intended to be our treasure, our most precious possession on this earth. It is true that our woman allow us to possess them now and then in that ultimate man-woman relationship. They were given to us not to own but to cherish, to protect, and to love, and to give honour to their sacredness. I think that is the way the Creator intended it to be so that we might live in harmony in His good way.

A woman was once a little girl who came from her father and her mother. She was like a pretty flower, kissed by the dew at night and wakened and loved by the sun each day. She was caressed by the gentle wind till she blossomed into the full beauty of her womanhood. Yes, she was a flower in the garden of the Creator and she was intended to produce more of her kind so that the garden could be filled with a harmony of colour and form.

These words are unfinished because the Creation is unfinished. There are always more babies to be born, more to do and more life to live and the wonder of the unfolding Creation to watch and think about. No woman has told me what is, nor written any words here. So I can only share with you from my limited understanding.

I do know that every woman is a mystery to herself because she is a part of the great unknown, the mystery of life. If a nation of people would rise and stand in their place in the sun they must honour their women first and help them to get up before any thing good can happen, but only the women can restore their own sacredness again.

There was a story about when the Creator made the first man. He made the man and He sat him on the earth. He watched him for a long time and He saw that the man was lonely and did not seem to be too happy about the way things were around him. He had no one to talk with, and alone he could not reproduce himself. So the Creator said "I can do better than that". So He made a woman, and He fashioned her in such a beautiful way, and He gave her to the man to be his mate. He created a perfect harmony of need and fulfillment. Each was suited to the other like it is in all the rest of the Creation. But now we see that that harmony is lost and there is a great sadness and a great agony because many of the women have their hearts torn out of them and all the hope and the promise that the Creator put into them has been ripped away.

Positive and Negative

I want you to consider well these two questions, positive and negative because they are the first and most fundamental facts of life for us. They are the questions we will deal with every day of our lives and if we come to understand them, there will be very little mystery about life. In fact we can go through life with a serenity and inner tranquillity that others will wonder about.

It is true of life that it is vastly complex but at the base of its great complexity is a very simple truth. That is why I ask you to consider the two questions positive and negative because that is vital to the way we relate to each other as people, and especially at this time in our relationships as male and female people.

When I speak of positive and negative I want to relate it to what we call electrical power, but I also want to relate it to the Creator and his opposite, the great Evil One.

In electricity there are two opposite principles which is a flow of positive and negative electrons and as long as they are kept separate like in two of three different wires or conductors then they have what we call *a usable potential* or *electricity*.

But if those wires are somehow crossed or short circuited then the positive electricity *goes to ground* and there is *no usable electricity*. They simply cancel each other out.

There are two opposite principles that we must recognize and constantly deal with as long as we live on this earth. I suppose we could call them opposite or warring factions, because they are always in opposition to each other! The Chinese people have what they call the yin and yang principles of life but I believe those are male and female principles which are opposites but which require each other for completion and fulfillment. I know that those principles are vastly more profound than the simple way I relate them here. I believe they were developed in order to understand the mysteries of life itself. If we can come to a satisfactory understanding of life then we have a chance to live life in a serene and true way, in tune with the universe. It's on that basis that we can build our philosophy of life. But that philosophy of life cannot be held by only a few individuals. It must become the common understanding of the people or it won't work.

It's like a beautiful element of life which is no good to us until we take it up as a common understanding and collectively use it.

If that is a true and logical kind of reasoning then we must come to understand what we are as the human element in God's vast Creation. But how will we come to understand what we are and what part was given to us in that ongoing Creation if we persist in using negative thinking?

Negative thinking is distorted thinking, positive thinking is true thinking.

It is obvious that the greatest power in the universe, the Creator, made us co-creators with Him but not quite in the same sense that He made the flowers and the growing things or the animal and the fish life, because they have no choice but to follow what we call the original instructions that He gave to them.

I say that He gave the same identical instructions to us as He gave to the plants and the animals but in addition He gave to us *a free will*, that is to say, He made us *flesh and spirit*, and that spirit being part of the Great Spirit is answerable to Him. And because we are flesh and spirit we have the need to nourish both the flesh and the spirit. Either one without nourishment will get sick or die that is why the great spirit power gave us both physical food and a way of spiritual nourishment. Either way we must be directly involved in getting that nourishment or we won't have it. That is why He gave each kind of people their spiritual way like the black, the white, the yellow and the red peoples.

I'm not going to try to make it more complicated than that because I want to try to share understanding not spread confusion. All I'm trying to do is to point out the road and if you follow that road you will come to your own understanding, which is the best way.

There are only two roads for us to walk on and we have to choose one or the other. I say that He gave the same identical instructions to us as He gave to the plant and the animal life on this earth. They are:

1. Self preservation

2. Reproduce our own kind.

Those instructions are sacred because the work of the Creation is sacred. If we carry out our part of that work then our part of the Creation keeps on going as it was supposed to.

In my way of understanding positive equates with the Creator, the great spirit power. All of His on-going Creation is life, animate and inanimate. It is the vibrating, pulsating universe in its endless incomprehensible variety, constantly the same, yet always changing. It contains birth and life and death. It contains love and hope and truth. It is the total reality of truth. It is truth in its invincible self. It is the Creator Himself, and there is no other power in the universe that is equal to his power.

That is the positive power that I am talking about.

Change is constant, it never stops, from the moment we are conceived in our mother's womb we begin a constant process of change that never stops, not even after we die.

Truth equates with the supernatural power who is the Creator. He is truth. His only working element is truth and the time will come when massive deception will be obliterated from this earth and only truth in its massive power will stand there. That will be after the purification of this earth is finished and only true things and true people will be seen there with Him.

Negative

The great evil power is the one that I call the great negative. His work is the destruction of all that is true and good. Massive deception is his only (working element). He has been called the great deceiver which is a true name for him.

Materialism is the opposite of spiritualism and materialism is the only goal of the great evil power. Power equates with evil or good and I say that if you control a lot of people you control a lot of power. If you control a lot of money you control a lot of power, and control of the money and the people and the resources of the earth is the exercise of power. And that is precisely what the dominant society is all about. As you are well aware the dominant society is "the white society".

The control of power is not evil or good in itself – it is simply a reality.

The dominant society is a materialistic society. Its god is money and the acquisition of material things. It is a negative society. It has been rightly called a death culture, and we can see very clearly now that wherever it touches its hand it brings death. It is a parasitic society, and like all parasites it has no other way but to devour its host.

A man gave me a dead sheep a few winters ago because I wanted the hide, and he said "I don't know what happened to it, it just died one day and that's all there was to it." So I took the sheep home and thawed it out and then I skinned it. I was a little worried that it might have died from some kind of sickness but when I took a careful look, I saw that there were so many sheep ticks in the hide that it had simply died from lack of its own blood because the parasites had simply destroyed the life that they depended on to keep their own lives going and when it dies they died too.

A sheep tick buries its head in its victim, which is the only way it can live and when its head is buried all it does is suck blood. That is the way of all parasites, they contribute nothing but pain and suffering. Their only way is devouring, a way of death that brings their own death.

In time of great purification those who follow that great negative way on this earth will be confronted with truth. Those who follow a materialistic culture will have no power over those who follow a spiritual way because truth and deception are incompatible. They will not be able to stand together on this earth.

Our mother earth will be renewed again and this earth will become a place of peace and good order, a place of life. And those who think and live and do in a negative way will find no place there, because like the parasites they will be eliminated from that true way, that true place.

Those are the elements of the battle that is going on now in this world between the two greatest powers in the universe. One is the great negative or evil power and the other is the great positive or creative power. The Great Mystery Himself, the Creator. And I ask each one of you who read this to think seriously about it and decide for yourself which side you are on, because there are only two sides. *There is no middle ground.* There are only two roads.

In the great war that is happening now all the people of the earth are on *one side or the other* either consciously or unconsciously. Because both those great powers are using people, not bombs and bullets, but people – you and me. They are using the ideas of positive or negative, good or evil, right or wrong, truth or deception. That is why it is important for us to decide which side we are on *now*. Only one of those great powers can win.

It seems like I have strayed a long way from what I set out to do, and that was to show how the men relate to our women people and that is because it is very obvious that our relationships are terribly out of balance now. It is also for the purpose of trying to restore the woman's power and how they see themselves, which to me seems to be a very profound question then we must look for a reasonably profound answer. That is why I asked you to consider the question of positive and negative. You may suppose that they are two entirely different and separate questions, but in life it seems to me that we cannot separate them. We can only consider them and deal with them, because like a revolution it is not what we like and it is not what we want, it is simply that *it is what it is*.

I say that negativism equates with materialism and I believe that because this great so-called civilization has always puzzled me with its laws and its police and its school system and its ways of death. I could never understand this terrible oppressive system until I began to understand the elements of positive and negative and to equate them with good and evil. It was only then that I began to see what this majority society is all about. And it is in the hope of helping others to see what it is that I write this.

The Great Negative

Women see themselves in a negative way because that is where it has got down to in these times that we live in. There is no mystery about womankind anymore. They are sexual playthings, they are things to be used, to sell cars, or soap, or a hundred thousand other things that the money makers must sell to maintain and expand their artificial world and get more and more power.

It's a long story and I would like to go back to 1929 when I listened to the advertisers who sold their flour on the basis of "This flour makes the whitest bread" and the women bought whatever flour made the whitest bread. So in order to make the whitest flour they ground it and they bleached it and they took every possible bit of food value out of it, and that was what the women fed their men and their children. And then to make up for the lost food value they ran to the doctors and the drug stores for pills and things to try to maintain the health of their families but that wasn't all, that was only the beginning. They also needed beauty aids to make up for the lost natural health so that the cosmetics industry too became a multimillion dollar business.

The women stopped making bread and all things. They got the baker to bring them to the door instead and all they had to do was exchange those goodies for money and then next morning they packed some of those *goodies* into a lunch can and sent *their slaves* out to get more money. And it was the women who made it possible for the convenience foods industries to build themselves into the gigantic monstrosities that they are today. And I say it was with the active participation of the woman that the food that was once pure and good, compared to the stuff that is sold as food today, was transformed into what is not fit for pigs to eat. So I ask you to think very seriously about who enslaved who?

Every dollar spent for non-food, convenience foods, is the most powerful vote that can be given to the manufacturers of those things. It was also the women who slavishly listened to the doctors who said women shouldn't nurse their babies. They should put them on a formula instead. Formulas that the doctors invented, then they prescribed how many ounces for each feeding and watched a clock to make sure that the babies were fed precisely on time *as the doctor said*. Common sense was thrown out with the garbage, and the woman allowed themselves to become enslaved to the stupidity that the doctors promoted.

So the women have had the biggest share in enslaving not only themselves but their men and their children; and, although it may be unfair, I have often wondered, with some degree of anguish, if the majority of women didn't believe that their heads were made only for the purpose of growing hair and keeping their ears apart. The majority of them obviously didn't do any serious thinking. Otherwise they would not have considered it a female prerogative to be frivolous and inconsistent about life.

Yes the women have let us down a hell of a long ways and they have no right to believe that it was the men alone who got them into the slavery that they are now in because it never could have happened without the passive and the active participation of the women themselves.

Do the women have a positive image of themselves? How could they when they have so actively participated in bringing everything to a negative way? And if that is so how could the men see them in anything but a negative way?

This is why I say that if we are going to find the true way again we must first help our women to get started on that way and we must support them and give them strength and encouragement because they cannot go anywhere without us, because without us they are nothing, just as we are nothing without them.

The Great Negative Society

The great negative society has created a totally artificial and negative environment, that is essential and necessary to its parasitic ways. The negative environment is fashioned by the power structure, that is the invisible government, consisting of those who control the economy of a country. As Baron Rothschild once said of the government of France "Give me control of the banks of France and I don't care what government the people elect". So the control of a country consists of the control of its economy or, as in a military dictatorship, by control of the people.

So there is an invisible government, a power that controls the elected government and the imperatives of that invisible government are progress and development, expansion and profits. It is the nature of that monstrosity the invisible government that it must always expand and grow larger at the expense of human progress and human development.

It is a totally negative and totally materialistic way. Its only god is materialism and every day human lives must be, and are, sacrificed to that God so we should not be too surprised that there's so much strife and unrest in the world.

From the very beginning in Canada up until now it has been the financial interests and the power barons of England and Canada and other countries that fastened their tentacles on the land and the forests and the water and the minerals of this land.

Like a giant octopus they stretched their tentacles all over this land and by using what was supposedly a democratically elected government they extinguished the rights of the original people who were here when they the thieves came and in order to keep what they had stolen. They made laws to make sure the original people never got their source of power, the land, back again.

It was for that reason that the federal police, the RCMP were set up and reserves (ghettoes) created. The federal police herded the people onto designated, usually barren land and made sure that they stayed there.

But a free people are a dangerous people to a monopolistic system and the capitalistic system is every bit as evil and monopolistic as the communist system is in Russia and the countries that Russia dominates. Only the methods are different, that's all. Both systems require thought control, only in this country they call it education. Aldoph Hitler used compulsory education too and look what he did.

Compulsory Education

The education system in this country is in reality indoctrination. It always was a system designed to promote the right values, the right sense of history and that history was British and European imperialist, conquest and domination. And so the system was for the purpose of teaching people how to run effectively on the economic treadmill either as producers and consumers or as exploiters. So the departments of education all had that same job no matter what government they were in or where they were located. And since they were a totally negative society dedicated to the pursuits of materialism, they could not teach anything else but what they knew. How else can anyone explain the anti-human way that the whole dominant society has gone?

I believe with some exceptions that the women saw themselves in a negative way, realizing subconsciously that the great mystery had given them special gifts and also a special purpose in his Creation, and it seems to me that they were somehow uneasy because somewhere along the way the true purpose and understanding had been lost and surely life wasn't given to us for the frivolous purposes like the majority of people seemed to show by their actions. But where is the understanding and what is truth?

It's into this situation that the boys were born and they grow up to be men learning that great negative way from the environment around them. We are conditioned by our environment just as surely as the trees and the plants and the animals are, and they learned in the same schools as the girls did and the schools always somehow conveyed a negative attitude about girls.

I suppose that in the dehumanizing process that was going on the most vulnerable part of the society had to be attacked first and that was the female element.

The churches also had a great deal to do in making women subservient second class citizens and keeping them that way till now. So the power structure had fashioned a total package which was primarily delivered by the school system and by the legal system and by every other means possible for the purpose of mental, spiritual and physical enslavement of the citizens of the country. A total way of freedom of choice. It reminds me of the hungry thirties when the billboards were covered with slogans to get the peoples minds diverted from their troubles.

They had slogans like "The only man who is better off is the one sitting on a tack". They also advertised about the great freedom we had. After many ways of trying to define that freedom some of us came to the conclusion that the only real freedom we had was *the freedom to do what we are told.*

So the boys grew into men in this great negative environment and they followed the way of the majority society and accepted their value system which put down human values and elevated material values. One of those principal values was personal pleasure, and foremost among those was drinking and complete sexual licence. Some people even said that God was dead because they had gone a long way down the wrong road. The predominant thinking seemed to be that women were sexual playthings which is a terribly wrong way of thinking.

So if we are going to get back to the right way again we will have to get involved with our own personal purification and spend each day preparing for the final purification that is very close now.

I believe that the preparation required of us is that we must restore our humanity to the greatest degree that is possible for each of us. To do that we have to turn to the Creator who made us and to our fellow human beings who have set themselves to do the same thing because we will need others help and encouragement always.

We must learn how to become positive thinking people. We must learn to differentiate between positive and negative and make a conscious decision which side we are going to be on. There are only two roads and we can only walk on one of them. The great river of life rushes on and there is so little time left.

THIS IS A DOCTORING SONG FOR NISHNAWBE WOMAN

March, 1983

Come sit with me Nishnawbe woman
  have a song to sing for you,
    It takes all night so don't be hurried
      Come sit by my fire across from me
        The sun has gone down, The stars are bright
          The moon has come up with her silver light
            So sit in peace while my water drum sings
           This healing song for you.

My woman, look
  Outside the door of my lodge.
Our mother rests
  Till the sun comes up
    But now the mist is rising.
Now go outside and feel that mist
  On your face and hands and body
    And smell its fragrance,
      It speaks of power and beauty and sacredness
        It speaks of woman,
          Sacred Female being.

Now come inside
  And we'll pray together.
To the fire we'll give our offerings,
  Of sage and cedar and sweetgrass and tobacco,
    Because we must give thanks
      For this healing song
        To the Medicine Power who gave it.

Now listen, quiet, while my water drum sings
  This song of love for you,
    Come look through my eyes and read in my mind
      And I'll show how I see
        What it means to be a woman.

Now the song begins
  But its hard to sing
    Because it talks of sorrow and greed and lies
     and desecration,
      And it talks of life and love
       And the woman's place in the history of her Nation.

Now here my woman is a gift for you.
I take it from my heart
  I kindle the fire within your breast
  And make it warm and bright
    So your spirit can rest and be in peace
     While your menfolk walk beside.
The gift I give you,
  It came from God.
It isn't mine to keep.

The gift He gives in this teaching.
He came to this man
  Who walked alone.
He said to me,
  "I'll have a gift to give to you
    She'll be your female partner
     and through her
      I'll give you children
       Like flowers in my garden".

"This gift I give you, You must always hold her precious
  Because without her you are nothing.
From her will come the Nations
  To fill this earth. And she will be the foundation,
    if she is strong
     and her mind is clear.
Then all will be in balance
  And all will be well."

"If she is weak
  and doesn't know her purpose,
    Then you will fall
     And the people will die.

Her rights, her gifts and all I gave her
   No one should take away,
      Because when the woman's heart
         is on the ground
            It's finished,
               There is no more to say."

He said
   "The woman's place and the work I gave her
      was for my sacred purpose,
         and if she leaves and goes astray
            Then no one has a purpose.
The children will cry,
   The men will be lost,
      And all will come to nothing".

He said
   "Here is my gift
      That I give to you:
         This woman.
I have made her place
   At the center of the circle of life,
      Let it always be that way
         and it will be well for you."

Thank you Grandfather
   That's how it should always be.
Thank you for this woman
   and for life.

So now my woman
   I have this question.
Why are you so concerned
   To go to that hill where they write the laws
      about equal rights for Indian women?
When you know these laws written on paper
   will mean nothing in the courts of law
      Just as it has always been?

What will it mean to Indian Nations
   If the laws are written
      As you know they should,
         But you know so little
            of what it means
               To be a woman?

Only God could make a woman
   And only God and woman can know what that means
      If you my woman
         Have lost the meaning.
Then its time to lay down and die
   Because life has no more purpose.

Why do you worry
   About laws and lies
      And courts and such
         When what we need
            To take our place in the sun
               is strong women.

We'll stand beside
   And help you
      We'll honour and respect you
         We'll defend your right
            To your woman-ness.
That way it can come back to balance again.

This is how
   My healing song ends.
Woman, you are entitled
   To respect
      As a child of God.
But in this mad world we live in
   You can demand respect,
      But you'll hardly ever get it.

Only when you have gone back
   And searched
      In the mind of God
         And in your heart

And the hearts of other women;
Only when you have found
The meaning of Woman,
Then will you come back.
and command respect.

Till then your man
and your children must wait,
How long?
My woman
How long?

Grandfather I give you thanks for women.
Give us strength and guidance
To find the ways
To heal ourselves
and our women.

Only God could make a woman.

NOTES ON THE PHILOSOPHY OF AN INDIAN WAY SCHOOL

It seems to me that at the heart of the philosophy of an Indian Way School there first has to be a connection with the spiritual because in the "Native" way of teaching and learning, there was first the Creator of the universe and all of the Creation of which we are a part. In the natural way of teaching we are taught that first there was the established order of the Creation with its purpose, and its harmony, and its sacred rhythms of which the days and nights and the returning cycles are a visible part, and of which birth and death are also a part.

So in the traditional ways of teaching there was as much concern for the meaning of life as there was for the fact of life as each person lived out their own allotted time.

There was a recognition that each human being as they came to live among us was a spiritual being as well as a physical person. That spirit being came from the spirit world and must eventually return to the spirit world, that is, back to the Creation from which it came. And because that is so then there had to be a total respect for that young one who just came to us.

The traditional respect was such that the leaders and the elders constantly reminded each other that no important decision was to be made without full consideration for the unborn, that is the faces of the ones coming toward us for seven generations into the future, for it was clearly understood by our people that we were not the owners of this land.

We were the "Keepers of the Land" for the ones to come after us. We were to keep it in trust for them and we were to keep it clean and not disturb its harmony or its cycles because it belonged exclusively to the One who created and maintained it. And we, his children were only visitors here in this part of the Creation. We were guests and we were to conduct ourselves in a sacred way.

It has always been clear in our minds that the natural things around us also had their own part in the ongoing Creation, their own original instructions. The plant life, the water life, the animal life, the bird life, our Mother Earth, our Grandmother Moon, our elder brother Sun, the star world – all these had followed their own original instructions.

The fire was sacred, the water was holy – it was not to be defiled but was to be respected and used for its healing and life giving power. The air provided life giving breath. The sacred powers of the four directions are still following their original instructions. Time has always belonged to the Creator and was to be measured by the Creation's rhythm, not by a treadmill system. Life was given to us to celebrate, not to endure.

We as Native people have traditionally been more concerned with human development as opposed to the development and acquisition of material things.

We as Native people have witnessed the almost total failure of the school system for us as a people, have come to the conclusion that it is time that we provide an education that has substance and meaning for us and our children. What we propose to do is to return to the ways of our people that has stood the test of uncounted centuries – a way that gave spiritual riches and and a sense and meaning and a purpose for life.

We propose to surround our children with a total educational environment whereby the teachers and the parents and the elders provide an education that is fashioned not only by those who teach but also by the ones who learn. We will again become each others teachers as it always was.

Because God "so loved the world" He did not send a school board or a department of education, He sent mothers and fathers and it was to them that He entrusted the continuing generations of little ones.

A talk with trainees at New Careers, Winnipeg, December 1983

WE CAN CHANGE THE WORLD BY STARTING WITH OURSELVES

As Natives, we must involve ourselves in changing the world we live in, we begin this by changing ourselves. We are called to care for ourselves and each other. We need to recognize that we are children of God. All effective change has to start with us. We can't change other people, they have their right to be who they are. We can help, but they are the one's who choose change. I must look at myself, who am I? Am I happy? Am I in control of my life? of my destiny? Am I going to fix me? I am called to care about my brothers and sisters. I am called to be a beautiful person, a caring human being. My teachers have been the earth, the fish, the animals, the trees, the wind, etc. We all need to find good people for we have a need for nurturing relationships.

We have desperate needs. There was a woman in prison I visited. Constantly throughout her life she had been told she was a bad girl. In her relationships, she needed to recognize that she was a beautiful person, like a jug if it is full you can pour some out for others; if the jug is empty you can't give to others. We're all children of God, beautiful human beings. As people we recognize ourselves. We must have nurturing relationships so that we can grow into that beautiful person we're called to be. It's like putting a plant out in the sun. It needs nurturing or it will perish. Like the woman in prison, she needed to find out who she was. Everything was cut off from her in prison. We all need to find out who we are. The things we want, we block. It took her a long time to see herself as a human being, it takes time and patience. She has been cheated out of being a little girl and also out of her childhood. In effect we are our own worst enemy. It's a gift of God to grow from little girls and boys. In growing we become deformed emotionally, physically, spiritually, intellectually. We don't know the forces that have acted on us.

Life teaches us a valuable lesson: You can never tell by the looks of a frog how far he can jump. We look, classify, make judgements, misjudge as we see others. This seems to be for self-preservation. We need to re-examine what we think and how we are.

In Cape Breton I saw how some trees were different and some were good, some natural and some deformed. When I saw them I told my son "It must be the soil". He said "No, its the weather." At the micro-wave stations the tops of trees looked like they were run over by a lawn mower. Sometimes the tops of trees are covered by a sheet of ice. The trees were conditioned by environment, a violent system. We are also effected by our environment and we can affect our environment. Do we produce a violent environment?

Education in North America is compulsory miseductaion. Education is conforming to the needs of the system. People are forced to conform to the system. We need to re-educate ourselves to free ourselves. Oppression of women is called liberation of women. Women as they become liberated will liberate their oppressor. We have to recognize that our people are hurting and desperate. Needs come from the Creator. Our needs need to be fulfilled or they produce reactions. We don't have to measure age by young or old – it's a state of mind. We have a life time to learn and to grow. Life teaches us that once, as we are born, we receive instructions and our lives are meant to fulfill in the same way that the plants, birds and animals also receive instructions. Once we are born we are to grow to our greatest beauty, spiritually, physically, emotionally, intellectually. We are to reproduce ourselves and our bodies will go back into the earth eventually. Just as with a plant: the seed falls; whether the seed grows is conditioned by rain, warmth and environment. In the arctic there are flowers just so high but in a different environment they grow higher. In an environment we can grow or get destroyed. That's why there are suicides, people are in an environment where they can not grow. We can't read their hearts. They self destruct because of their environment.

When I worked for Ontario Hydro-Electric, I saw where they put pavement down, where they funnelled water away from hydro stations because the water that wanted to go back where it came from posed a danger to the electricity. I saw some lumps under the blacktop and wondered about them. They got bigger but did not break out. If I was to open the lumps I would find plants all curled tight. The plants were trying to grow but their life force was working against the oppressing force: if they persisted in their growth the plants would self-destruct; if they resisted less or more passively they might obtain some freedom.

We wonder why youth act so strangely and commit suicide. They are prevented from growing to their greatest beauty, physically, spiritually, emotionally and intellectually. This is their right from the Creator. They realize that their inheritance is stolen. At the World Council of Churches there was a youth projection. They said, "You tell us we're the church of the future but we're people who don't see the future. There isn't any future. Its been stolen." These are the dynamic plants who can't grow or they will self-destruct.

Education created artificial reality. They say "It's a dog eat dog society. It's not the way we like it but that's the way it is." We don't have to accept this – we have the opportunity, the right and the responsibility to change this thinking. We are called to assist at the birth of a new world. Individually we must do something for us. We must stop destroying Creation, the earth, and it's people. Those who destroy Creation destroy the earth. What can I do? The only thing I can do is to do something about me. I am the one who willingly and unwillingly destroys earth by wanting more and more.

Paper towels we use only once as opposed to a rag that can be used again and again. There is incredible waste and there is no end to it. We have to cut more trees to produce more paper towels or stop cutting trees for this sort of thing. We will walk into a new day. Be conscious of waste. We can contribute to making a better world. We can become real people, the artificial will be destroyed despite all the powers that force against us. This is God's Creation. He or she is still in control.

In the spirits there is a sense of urgency of things. We hope to do things differently. It's a new day. We need to sit down by ourselves in God's presence and ask Him who are we? Why are we here? What is a purpose for my life? What does it mean to be a man or woman? God is love, He loves us. We have to believe in ourselves and in God. In a World Council of Churches conference, the focus was on the meaning of life. I was present as a Native Spiritual Elder. I asked how can we expect to answer. "What is the meaning of life" when the other half of the question is not asked, "what is the purpose of life?" There is a purpose and it is sacred and precious. We have to understand that we have opportunity, responsibility and the power to change the world. The whole system told us we are powerless. It is not true.

Systems such as the correction system are based on violence, hatred and revenge. This is wrong. It's an abomination in the face of God. It must be removed. I will not leave it the way it is.

It matters for each of us that the little bit we put in is positive. The Creator is with us. The positive power says no to violence, hatred, revenge. We are called to affirm life for us. If there is no justice there is no peace. Neither Reagan, nor the Russians have any right to do what they are doing. The nuclear holocaust will result in total destruction. We have a fouled mess on our hands. We must start to create again, nurture and care in a relationship now. We have power, love, and care about ourselves. We can create a new world by starting with ourselves.

Men are both male and female, women are both male and female. In order to be more complete human beings we have the opportunity to help understand. God created beautiful human beings not garbage. The Spirit's are working overtime we have the opportunity to experience it. There will not be a Third World War.

We must be on the positive side of the struggle. The beast is losing his power. Why are we here? Let's begin to affirm life of ourselves and each other. Like the plant, animal system we've been given original instruction. We can play with trinkets or choose life. Every human being is a child of God. This is a dangerous and exciting time to be living, yet what is possible now wasn't possible a few years ago. One of my major thrusts is to empower people, make them realize that power does not come from the Government, the mouth of a gun. But our power comes from the Creator directly to each individual. He gave us gifts, destiny, power – that's the vital element. We need intellectual liberation to liberate ourselves from the miseductaion and misunderstanding we received. We have to really understand why we are here. Our only way to serve the Creator is to serve our fellow man, then I can be happy with who I am. It requires time and patience. As I exercise I become more expert. We need to empower people, it's the most important thing – people helping people believe in themselves.

The reason women are more vulnerable is that they are nurturing by nature. Their femininity is diminished by not nurturing. Men can learn to nurture. It is the fullness of their manhood to accept themselves as male and female. The action of two elements can continue. Our Creator is both male and female. We develop our fullness, it takes time. For women gossip is malicious – when you put people down you put yourself up. When men act tough, he-man, they deny part of themselves where people see their beauty. It is artificial. It is destructive. Their way of seeing the world would be richer. I feel compelled to help women to be who they are called to be. Yet only women can liberate themselves. We need to be patient with ourselves; then, learn to be patient with others.

CHAPTER SIX

Stone Walls and Prison Bars

Art's own spiritual journey was radically transformed by his work bringing traditional spiritual services to Native inmates in prisons around Ontario. He began to visit the prisons in the mid '70's, about the time that Native brotherhoods and sisterhoods were first beginning to take shape.

At that time, traditional ceremonies such as the Sweet Grass ceremony and sweat lodges were unknown and effectively prohibited in both federal and provincial institutions. Art's earliest prison work was in the provincial prisons such as Guelph. Later he became convinced that the places where the people were in the greatest need of support and counseling was the federal institutions such as those in the Kingston area.

Nonetheless, in the early years the provincial prisons presented a problem of their own. When "Native Brotherhoods and Sisterhoods" started to take form in the federal institutions, the provincial authorities went far out of their way to make sure that no such thing happened in their institutions. Indeed, Native inmates in Guelph were able to meet together only under the sponsorship of the Catholic chaplain of the day. Only after several years of spiritual subterfuge were they allowed to form their own organization, and then only with the spiritual nicety of distinguishing themselves from a "brotherhood" by taking on the name of "Native Sons."

His early work in the federal institutions often frightened and disturbed Art. He found he needed to gain sufficient trust from the authorities to exercise the same freedom of movement as other chaplains. More important, he needed to gain the trust of the inmates who came to see him as a Native elder, a person whose role was really similar yet very different from that of a Christian chaplain.

Art has devoted particular attention to the Native women at the Prison for Women in Kingston. Because "P4W" is the only federal prison for women in Canada, Native women are brought from all corners of the country. The factors of distance and poverty combine to completely isolate these women from their families, particularly from their children. P4W is a maximum and medium security institution. Where the men who come into the Kingston area might hope to work their way out of the maximum security environment into medium and minimum security settings, and can also hope for some proximity to their families, the women are placed in a situation which evokes despair and hopelessness. Art has devoted countless hours to providing a spiritual framework in which these women might find comfort and support to endure the time these women must serve while also trying to find relief for their intolerable condition.

Art has been at the forefront, over a period of more than fifteen years, of the battle to allow the full range of traditional Native spiritual ceremonies to be a part of the counseling and support available to Native inmates. While the authorities have long bemoaned the disproportionate number of Native people incarcerated throughout North America, they have also expended inordinate energy ensuring that traditional spiritual counsel – including ceremonies, prayer, ritual, elder's teachings and the opportunity for sustaining contact among Native inmates – would remain unavailable.

Even when Native elders such as Art began to be welcomed into the institutions and given chaplain's status, the opportunities for Native inmates to practice their own traditions remained severely limited. At times, in the absence of an opportunity to offer sweet grass or to burn tobacco in a proper ceremony, Art has taught inmates to leave a cigarette burning in an ashtray and meditate quietly while focusing on the rising smoke. Imagine, if tobacco were available for use as a sacred offering but no longer used in its addictive and debilitating forms!

More important to Art is to imagine and to focus people's attention on the reality that Native people, at the time of first contact by Europeans had no prisons at all while today they represent the largest single population in prisons in almost every jurisdiction in North America. Art's own meditations and reflections on this state of affairs reflect his hurt and outrage at the devastation of his people which began with the residential schools and the children's aid's wholesale removal of children from their natural settings and is continued in the institutions of higher incarceration.

– m.p.

UNIVERSAL WOMAN

January, 1985

My little sister
I see you crying
I feel your hurt
I share your sorrow
You're in prison
Oh God forbid.

The Children's Aid
They stole you
From your mother
When you were only little

Oh God, yes
I know them well;
Those white Christians
With their uppity standards;
Oh God, have pity on their souls
When their time comes;
And God have pity while you're at it
On us, the victims
Of a vicious law-abiding society.

My little sister
I see you crying
I feel your hurt
I share your sorrow;
Oh, the C.A.S.
They stole your children too?

Oh God have pity
On your children and you,
Those uppity bastards
And their holy standards

My little sister
Did no one ever tell you
That God never created garbage?

Did no one ever say
That within you
Is a beautiful human being?
The one that God created
In Her own image and likeness?

Yes, my little sister
Only God could create a woman
So beautiful, so complete.
But here you are in prison
So destitute, so forlorn, so unloved;
Surely this is a strange planet
That we live on;
Oh God,
When will this blasphemy end?
Surely this was not your plan
That women should be locked
In iron cages
Behind stone walls.

Yes, my little sister
What can I do to ease your hurt?
And today I heard from your own lips
That the warden of this prison
Wanted to celebrate
The fiftieth anniversary
Of this place of stone and steel and living hell
Oh God, what kind of perverts
Run these awful places.

Oh God, have pity on us your children,
The Native people of this land;
We were a prisonless society
But now we fill their jails
To overflowing;
Have pity on racist judges
Because their time will come
As surely as tomorrow
When your way will be done
On earth
As it is in heaven.

So now my little sister
What words of comfort can I say?
You spoke of suicide
Oh God, no;
You spoke of justice
Of which little shows;
Well I have another story
And this is how it goes.

A woman said to me one time
This is how I understand:
They say God created man
And put him here on earth
Like all His creatures free
And then He watched him every day
To see how he would be.

The man was lonely and forlorn
With no way to see how
To reproduce himself;
No love, no affirmation;
So God He turned in to himself and said:
This just can never be.

A woman, He created
And said to man:
I've brought you a gift
She'll be your partner
For now and ever.

This woman I give you
To cherish and love
She'll be your affirmation
She's my most sacred gift to you
The mother of all nations;
She is
Universal Woman;
Let her be the centre of your life
As she is the centre and purpose
Of all Creation;
That is the place I give her,
Let it be so
And walk in peace.

So now my sister let me say
The time of prisons will have an end;
It's marked so clearly by the hand of God
These cursed places
Of abomination
The God of all Creation
Will not let them stand
One stone upon another;
The dream of God
Does not include the hatred
Of one human against another.

"Justice, justice", did they say?
A lie, a monstrous evil lie
That's what it always is
And the rich they make the laws
That the poor ones have to live by;
They hide their evil doings
And said yours is the crime
But a scapegoat's what you are;
They've put their sins upon your head
And sent you to the desert,
A desert of stone and iron cages
Where hate is the only diet.

Oh God, have pity,
But didn't you say once long ago
Thou shalt love thy neighbour as thyself?
I though that's how you said it
But here on earth it doesn't show.

But what's to say now, little sister?
There still is more I'd like to share;
The evils of the prisons
Are not in the plan of God
They're simply a measure of control
Used by the rich against the poor;
The motto is:
To serve and protect,
Is that really so?
Yes, to serve those who have
And, to protect them

From those who haven't;
Oh God, have pity on us who haven't.

But still I must say more,
They say of Him who gave us life,
A day will come when we will stand
And only just one question He will ask
The same for you and me and others;
And to those who sent you to this place of shame
The only question there can be is this:
What have you done
With your time,
And the gifts
And the opportunities
That I gave to you?

"Justice, justice" they will say
In the courts of law
Justice is dispensed by the laws of man;
But how do you spell that, He will say?
J.U.S.T.I.C.E.?
No, they'll have to say
It's spelled j.u.s.t. u.s.
Then hang your head in shame
For you have dispensed your justice
Even in my name;
You sent my poor ones to your living hells
So now to you the same
You lying hypocrites,
No more will you play your games.

So now my sister let me say
I hear the drum
And the sacred songs
The heart beat of Creation;
They're calling you and me, my sweet
To build a new Creation.
I love you little sister,
I always did.

So take my hand and walk beside me,
Come my sister we must dance
We'll dance together in this dance of life;

Don't worry sister if you don't know how
Just walk beside me and you'll learn
Cause my job is to teach to you
How to celebrate life *together*.

So dry your tears my little sister
Put on your prettiest smile,
You are beautiful my little sister
And you are part of
Universal women,
And I am your brother.

THE BASIS OF LAW CONFLICT

It is through the total breakup of family life
   and having lost our original instruction
      that our people have become victims
         of a vicious system.
Robert Jaulin, the French anthropologist says of that system:
   "We are a civilization
      of vultures and parasites
         and we will end up eating
            our own decaying flesh."

The way back to restored dignity
   and pride for Native people in our own unique humanity
      is through the door that we came out of.
We have become a spiritually deformed people
   and only by returning to the sacred ceremonies
      that were given to us by the Creator
         can we again find the meaning and purpose for our lives.

A VISION FOR NOW

October 1984

About twenty-five years ago I was sitting
  At my kitchen table
    Not thinking or doing anything in particular
     And this is what I saw.

Way off in the distance
  Beyond the reach of human eyes
  I saw a set of scales.
They measured the weight of evil and good
  Or the weight of negative and positive.
The scales weighed down on the negative side,
  They couldn't go down any further.
There seemed no hope for human life
  The negative was the winner.

But from out of somewhere
  Came a human hand.
It contributed to the positive
  And out of heaven came the hand of God
  And contributed something more;
  Then more hands came
  And made their contribution.
Each time the hand of God put more again
  And the scales began to change.
They changed so fast,
  Like almost a bolt of lightning.
The positive won.
There's nothing more to say except
  That good will triumph over evil.
  That is particularly true right now;
  About us and the time we are living in.
A small part of the human family
  Has stolen the inheritance of most of the rest
  of God's Children.

So they starve and they die or they are liquidated.
  But they'll work and they'll struggle
  Until they are liberated
  By their hands and
  By the hands of God.
It just can't be any other way.
So beware oppressors
  Your time is marked.
You cannot keep it going.

I cannot bring myself to believe
  That God intended for any of His children
  To be locked in iron cages
  Behind stone walls
  Or shot and killed in cold blood
  By prison guards
  Or police.
And the anger locked inside our young people
  Is justified, *totally justified,*
  Because their right to life,
  Their right to collect their inheritance
  Is stolen.
If they are the children of God
  And if they are part of the God who created them as I believe,
  Then *their anger is the anger of God.*
  And the older and supposedly wiser ones
  Have no right to scold them for it.
Our young people are screaming their silent
  Screams at us.
Are we too blind to hear?
They are saying:
  "We want a new world,
  But we want it right now."
Our job is to help them unleash that anger
  In creative ways.

If we don't have the courage or the vision
  Then we better stand back,
    To hell out of the way.
Part of their power is their impatience.
  We should have the will and the courage
  To add our own.

Time will not stand still and wait for us.
This vision that came was a message
  That speaks to this time right now
  When everything seems so hopeless
  And the chances for peace so poor.
It was meant to give us hope and courage
  At a time when almost the only answers that we get
  From leaders and captive state governments
  Is to lock ourselves into a dance of death,
  The purpose seems to be
  That it's more important to celebrate death
  Than to affirm and celebrate life together.

It seems like they want us to celebrate "death"
  Not only for the whole human family
  But for all this part of Creation.
This vision says that for every small positive
  Contribution that we make
  The Creator puts His share in too.
It distresses me no end that so many pray to God
  And ask Him-Her to do this and do that, but seem not to
  Understand that our part is to be God's hands and feet
  And voice.
Our part is to get up and change the world.
It comes from the hearts and minds and hands of the
  Children of God who affirm Life for all that is living.

Their colours are black, red, yellow and white.
They are engaged in the dance of liberation,
  And the name of the power that they are using
  Is called L. O. V. E.
The invincible, irresistible power of God,
  Which He shared with us as one of our many gifts.
But it will do no good unless we use it.

Yes, we must engage in the dance of life.
We must liberate ourselves from stifling institutions
  And begin to celebrate our humanity together.
Because life was not given for us to endure
  But to celebrate.

And God's dream for us will not be accomplished
   By hiding in our little dark corners
   And shaking in our boots.

Listen to the teachers, the young ones.
They're saying we want a new world,
   But we need it *right now.*
Do we need to wait and talk about it first?
Or just get up and do it?
Time will not wait for us
   And those involved in the game of death
   Could get us hooked
   Because it's the only "game around."

I have an abiding faith in the God
   That I pray to;
   That He is not going to allow His Creation
   To be destroyed by the hands of Fools.

THE WINNING COMBINATION

January 1985

The winning combination, for us who have been taught
For so many lifetimes how to play the losing combinations,
is to learn to play the game of life by new rules,
Rules that we make for ourselves based on the old
Concepts of sacredness and human worth.
Not on the sanctity of money and personal possessions
But on the sacredness of Life.
I cannot believe that God ever intended
For any of His-Her children to be locked
In iron cages behind stone walls.
If that is the law of humanity
Then surely it is a symbol
Of humanity's total disregard for the laws of God.
Humanity has put aside the laws of Creation
That all life abides by.
Not only did they put the laws aside
But they put God on a shelf.
Then when they need Him-Her they go over to that shelf
And pray for what they want.
Meanwhile their hearts and their minds and their lives
Are dedicated to another God.
Who the hell do they think they are fooling?
In one country they write on their money,
"In God we trust",
And sure enough, there's His picture on the money.

LETTER TO AN INMATE AT MATSQUI INSTITUTION, ABBOTSFORD, B.C.

Dear Elmer:

Thank you for your letter. It was very beautiful in terms of its vital concern for Native people and the situation they find themselves in right now.

I have read your letter over and over again. I've shown it to two brothers who've just got out of the same kind of places. Just after I got your letter, I brought it to a Native studies class at the university. I read it to them and talked about it. Then a carload of us Native people left for Toronto, Hamilton and Guelph. We were gone four days. In each place we gathered people and had a sacred pipe ceremony. The last one was a prison where we've been three times now. There is a lot of demand for our help here and there. So much that we are working at absolutely top speed. I just finished a letter at 2:30 am this morning to a little sister of mine in Big Cove N.B. I met her in November in Quebec and she wrote a letter which was a desperate cry for help for her and her Dad and a few others who are searching for the true way in that place. I feel sure that some powerful help went to them from our prayers.

I do not know if this letter can get through to you or not. I will be writing to our brother Leonard Peltier as soon as possible and sending him some of the sacred tobacco. In those sacred pipe ceremonies that we have there is always someone including myself who are praying for our brothers and sisters in prison and for some who are being tortured and killed and its the same way when we pray with the sacred tobacco.

I have thought a lot about the questions in your letter and the most desperate and urgent question is a cry of anguish for unity among Native people along with a powerful concern for the future. What is the future? When does it begin? What does it hold?

The future is already arranged for the human family by the Creator. In other words, the destiny of man at this time has already been decided long ago the Creator saw that we would go a foolish way and that the time would come when He would have to purify His Creation here and start it again. At that time He will renew His original instructions to His children. He will use as *seed people living now*, young and old, of the four sacred colours of man *will be that seed* because that's how short the time is. Read the Revelation to St. John in the Bible. We keep telling our people whenever we can that we have still a short time to work at our own purification but most of them won't believe us.

They're the same ones you're talking about – the ones who don't care, who don't see and can't hear. They will be destroyed along with all those who follow that strange god, the one whose ways are the ways of lies and deception – the god whose ways are of money and materialism.

Look at who follows those ways. You will see that there is hardly anyone who sincerely tries to live in harmony with the Creation. There is positive and negative – those are the two greatest powers of the universe. One is good, one is evil. One builds, one destroys. One is the Creator, the other is called the Great Evil One. He has control over the vast majority of the human family and they are the ones who have the power over the lives of so many of us today. They have the laws and the institutions that are used to destroy us while they steal our inheritance all over the earth. Their system is money – that is the source of their power, money – and their leader is the great evil one.

There is a war between the great evil one and the Creator and only one can win – both are using the members of the human family. They are not using guns and bombs. The Creator has so few on His side so we go through a very heavy punishment because even our brothers and sisters ask us how come we are so stupid. This is a war for the hearts and minds of men. It is a war to destroy the Creation that our lives depend on or to preserve and restore the peace and harmony and the balance of the Creation.

This is very near to the end of that war. The evil one sees that he is already beginning to lose and there's no way he can win so he's more vicious and violent. He gives his orders to those who follow him and that's how they are as we see them go about their work. What is happening is that the system is coming apart. Cities and states and provinces are going bankrupt but they are still able to hide most of it from us. The money system is going to die. There is no other way and there is absolutely nothing they can do about it. Neither is there anything they can put in its place. They cannot face up to that and they are desperate. Read Alvin Toffler's little book called the *Eco-Spasm*. He is just one of those who predict that the money system cannot last beyond five years. My calendar says that there will be total chaos within the space of five years. When money dies who will pay the doctors and the firemen, the police and the armies with their guns? Who will buy in the supermarkets? Who will sell the oil and who will buy it? What will they do then? How will they divide and conquer us, in disunity, as they have done for so long now? Not only will they have no more power to harm but a great destruction will be sent to destroy all that is evil till all of the earth is clean and pure again. That is the great purification that the Indian prophesies tell us about for so long now.

What we are supposed to be doing now is our own personal purification while we wait for that time to come. Almost no one will believe that the Creator is looking in our hearts and minds to see which way we have decided to go. That's what's important - what's in our hearts and minds.

I've listened to the many anguished cries for unity and I've watched for a long time; and as I thought about your concerns, I came to the understanding that the only way for us to accomplish the unity we so desperately need is *through a triangle*. I have seen it working now many times. I have seen the only unity possible to us in action. It is still very weak but it is getting stronger. It comes only through the sacred pipe *when we pray with it sincerely*. It comes through the sweat lodge and the tobacco burning, the sacred ceremonies that were given to us - they include those brothers and sisters *who are in prison* as we pray for them.

All these ceremonies are only a part, the other part is that *we must pray individually* through sacrifice. There is a price and all of us wherever we are can pay our share towards that because it is done voluntarily with our hearts and minds. That is what the Creator is looking for.

Either we must follow in that evil way, the way of hatred and greed or we choose the other way, the sacred way. There is *no neutral ground*, - negative or positive that's all there is. And there is no time for us to form those normal human alliances and associations that were always so good for us. There is a great power against us that has every possible way blocked off and if we find another way it will block that off too because it is a great evil spirit power that sees and gives the directions.

If we want to become of one heart and one mind there is only one way left and it cannot be blocked off by anyone except each of us for ourselves individually. That triangle that I mentioned is both vertical and horizontal. It includes all the Creation and it includes all of us, but only if it includes the Creator can it include us. There are no boundaries.

There are no walls that can contain it or stop it. It transcends all boundaries and obstacles. Nothing can stop it but us individually *for ourselves*. The ideas and ideologies that divide us are like fog before the hot sun. I have seen this power in action in the last few months. It is still weak but as we practice with it , it will become very strong.

I have always been a fool because I believe this way and I try to live it. I cannot say any more except that this is the kind of fool that I am. Sincerely, your brother in suffering,   *A. S.*

International Conference on Prison Abolition – April, 1983: *Comparative responses to nonsocial behaviour by Native nations in their communities.*

HOW IT WAS THEN AND HOW IT IS NOW

The prison system in North America
is a blasphemy
in the face of God.
Is it an abomination. It calls itself
A correctional system, but it corrects nothing;
If it does anything it builds hatred and it smashes
Human beings.
It barefacedly says it "warehouses bodies".
It is a lie made manifest.

The prison system in Canada is an abominable beast
And I propose to address it in those terms.
I dare to stand toe to toe and stare in its
Evil face and address it as the evil that it is,
For in no other way can it be properly addressed
And dealt with.

The prison system is a beast that requires
Human sacrifice daily on its altar.

It is perhaps the only growth industry
In the land and what is happening now
Is that the system is building a bomb.
By doubling and tripling the number of prisoners
In cells too small for even one person;
As the bomb is built there is only one end result:
It will blow up in the faces of those who build it.

A friend in Kingston said a short time ago:
"Don't talk to people in terms of morals or human misery,
Talk to them *only in terms of dollars.*"
I say that:
As long as there are prisons there will be victims.
And as long as there are victims there will be injustice.
As long as there is injustice
There will be no peace on earth.
Only fools would dare to ask God

For peace on earth
While they actively and deliberately
Deny peace and justice
To their fellow human beings,
Men, women and children.

I would like to point out that we, the Native nations of this land
had no prisons!
We lived here for hundreds of thousands of hears
In our uncivilized pagan ignorance.
The land and the water and the air and all
The Creation belonged to God and we knew that.
We did not put fences around what we could not own.
Sure, we were not perfect,
But we had one essential quality that seems
To be largely abolished from the majority of society
We live with on this land that people call Canada.
That quality might best be expressed as
"Thou shalt love thy neighbour as thyself. "
And thou shalt love and honour thy Creator;
We did not talk about these sacred precepts
Nor did we write them in books,
We lived them.

For that reason we loved and honoured
The littlest child
To the oldest person
As a spirit being
In the flesh:
A child of God
With rights and responsibilities
And a personal vision
From God.

If we could not *own*,
Then no one could steal from us.
Sure, as nations we had territorial imperatives
Just as the animals and the birds and the fish
And the plants do;
And that was reason for conflict.
But that conflict derived from the life force itself,
Not from greed or the need for power over others.

Sure, we had deviant behaviour,
But we all belonged to each other,
And we were all responsible for each other.
We respected everyone's vision
About how they were to conduct their own lives.
And having that understanding
And that responsibility
We had also the right and the imperative
To personally work at correcting whatever
Was deviant from childhood.
We did not wait till a man or a woman was grown
And then try to make corrections,
Because we had no place to make those corrections,
And at no time in our history did we invent ways
To distort and deform the humanity of others.
And it was never known among us
That we blamed the victims for being victimized
As Christians have always done.

There is a fundamental difference
Between the people who belonged to this land
And the strangers who came here,
And that is a difference of philosophy.
One was based on the concept of materialism.
The other was based on the power and the beauty,
The sacredness, the timelessness and the harmony
And balance of Creation.

Yes, we were the uncivilized ones,
We were the pagans
But we had no prisons.
And the people always knew
That power
Comes from God,
Not from governments.
But to people,
Not to be given away
Because it corrupts
When it is used unwisely.
Because each one's responsibility
Was to God through His people.
And the ultimate punishment that could be given

By the people
Was banishment from the community
Because we had no prisons.

If the civilized Christians
Had only known
That the impossible transcendent answer
Always was:
"Thou shalt love thy neighbour . . .",
Not in words
But in deeds.

Just that one sacred precept alone
Would make it impossible
To have prisons
And if there were no prisons
There could be peace on earth.

Let them make bricks
With their hands.
They won't need guns
For that.

*Written for and delivered to the world community at Vancouver for the vigil
to remember the bombing of Hiroshima and Nagasaki.*

THE WHEELS OF INJUSTICE

They say that,
The wheels of "Justice,"
  They grind slowly.

Yes we know.

But they grind
And they grind
  And they grind
  And they grind.

It seems like they grind
Forever.

    And what they grind
    Is Human Beings,
    And how they grind.

They grind away
The Humanity

    Of the victims
    Who get caught
    In its jaws,

Oh God protect us
From a "law-abiding society;"

    Have pity on us
    Who are its victims,
    Protect us Oh God
    From those who say
    "We are Christians,"
    Because we know
    That if Christ
    Walked visibly among them today
    They'd throw Him in jail tomorrow,
    Oh God protect us from law abiding citizens.

The wheels of injustice
They grind forever,

> But they have nothing at all, to do with Justice,
> Because
> The
> Name
> Of
> The
> Game
> Is Vengeance.

Oh God protect us
From

> The
> Game
> Called
> Justice,
> Where the rich get richer
> And the poor
> They go to jail.

Yes the wheels of injustice
They grind so slowly

> And Human Sacrifice is their meat,
> They grind the hopes and the dreams of some
> While the parasites live in their homes of plush
> Oh God we are poor,
> Have pity on us
> And protect us from the Law Abiding Citizens
> Who turn the Wheels of Injustice.

CHAPTER SEVEN

A Song of Association

The prophetic voice faces no greater challenge than the challenge of association. This is the challenge that is faced when the visionary seeks the vehicle through which the vision might be realized. The loner who is content simply to give voice to his ideas becomes an artist, a writer, a singer. He seeks a safe haven from which his vision can be shared but also protected.

Alas, the time comes when the only way to be true to the vision is to leave the safe haven and brave the storms that ensue when we enter into association with others. Perhaps that is why the association that has held Art's devotion longer than any other is one which began its corporate life by saying that it would vote itself out of business when Native organizations had come into their own.

The present day C.A.S.N.P. has had two previous lives. In its first incarnation it was known as the Indian Eskimo Association (I.E.A.), a name which particularly belies the period of its founding in that its role at that time was to bring together people of good will from all walks of life who were prepared to hear the hopes and aspirations of Native leaders.

With the founding of the National Indian Brotherhood and the Native Council of Canada, the role of the I.E.A. came severely into question. At a national conference in 1972, after much soul searching, a consensus emerged that there was a continuing need for a charitable, non-political organization that would continue to provide a meeting ground for Indian and Native people and their non-Native friends and supporters. This role was re-affirmed a few years later when C.A.S.N.P. changed its name from the "Canadian Alliance in Support of Native People" to the "Canadian Association in Solidarity with Native Peoples".

The inter-cultural, non-partisan, grass roots nature of C.A.S.N.P. made a natural forum for the ecumenical message that Art Solomon brings to the world from his own Ojibway Nation.

This chapter begins with a poem, *Who is My Brother's Keeper* because that question goes to the very root of the challenge of association. That poem is followed by two pieces dealing specifically with C.A.S.N.P.: a statement of purpose which Art prepared during a critical point in the organization's life and a poetic reflection on the natural ways of the traditional peoples of the world.

The second is a meditation which Art wrote for a training programme for counsellors and leaders at the Burwash Native People's Project, a camp intended to be a place where Native youth could come, from prisons and from the streets of the city to learn the natural ways of their own traditions.

Commitment to Survival is also about the purpose of association. It speaks of a contract which people sign on coming into association, a statement that connects each individual's being with the larger being of a brotherhood, a sisterhood and a community. This chapter also contains two pieces which Art wrote in the Burwash Native People's Project.

– m.p.

WHO IS MY BROTHER'S KEEPER?

For that matter
Who is my Brother?

And what does it mean
when it was said

"Thou shalt love they neighbour
as thyself"?

Are those only words that were
given to be written in a book
and laid away somewhere?

Or were those sacred
principles that were given
to be lived by?

And by the way,
what is the weight of a snowflake?
and the dove answered the coal mouse,
"A snowflake weighs nothing more than nothing."
Well in that case
the coal mouse said,
"I must tell you an interesting story."
He said, "I was sitting on a branch
and it was snowing, ever so gently,
not harsh or hurriedly
but ever so gently,
and having nothing better to do
I counted the snowflakes as they
landed on my branch.
As I counted to four million nine hundred
and seventy-nine I thought, how gentle
and how pretty they look.
Then I counted four million nine hundred
and eighty and the branch broke."
The coal mouse looked up
at the dove who was so very wise
because he had been on the
ark with Noah.
Yes he was very old and very wise
but he had no answer
so the coal mouse flew away.

Yes, I have borrowed this story
from someone who had borrowed
it from someone else
who had borrowed it from someone
else, but it's so pretty
and it tells you what I want
to say.

Last November 18, 19, 1980
The Canadian Association in Support
of Native Peoples (C.A.S.N.P.)
held an annual meeting
in Winnipeg.
That meeting was different
because C.A.S.N.P. was at the point
of bankruptcy and it no longer
had a vision or a reason for being,
it seemed to me that the question
being asked was:
Shall we somehow attend to
the death of C.A.S.N.P. and try
in some way to give it a decent burial?

Or do we have the vision and
the courage to look beyond
this apparent disaster?
Is the work all finished?
or is there still much more to do?

I was reminded of the good Samaritan,
the priest and the Levite had passed this
desperately hurt human being and didn't care
a damn, but along came this poor one
and because of all his compassion he had no choice
but to give all the help that he could,
it was that choice that was made
at that meeting.

When that choice had been made
there was an election,
and ten directors were chosen
for an interim period of one year

They had been given the responsibility
of *searching for a vision*
And bringing C.A.S.N.P. out of bankruptcy,
we were also to find a new name
and a reason for being.

Of those ten directors three were chosen
and called "A Vision Committee".

The Vision Committee laboured hard
for months and now it is June 1, 1980
and it appears that we may have found
the vision and the reason for being.

The vision that we see has not been
accomplished by three people
but by ten directors
and if we are humble and wise
we will present the results of our work
to the people with humility
when the time comes.

The vision of the future work of what
is still called C.A.S.N.P.
may be with Native people in the prisons
and it may include other things.
We, as the present directors, have been
given this work to do
and when the time comes perhaps in a few
months we will say what we think
and others must make the choice.
Maybe someone else will be more specific
about the work we have done up 'till now
I hope so.

ANNUAL MEETING OF THE CASNP

The annual meeting of the Canadian Association in Support of Native Peoples in 1978 had to face directly the question of the relevance of CASNP and whether it should continue to function.

After much deliberation the assembly voted unanimously against a motion to dissolve. In so doing they not only acknowledged that the many problems that have plagued the organization in the past few years would be overcome but they also asserted beyond any doubt that at this present time in Canadian society there is a definite need for a group of people, Native and Non-Native, as equals, to directly address themselves to the problems that have been imposed onto Canada's First People by an aggressive dominant society.

We wish to reaffirm the fact that there are issues that affect all Canadians, whether they are Native or not, and that the provision of paternalistic, although well-intentioned, support groups are no longer needed.

What is required is a co-operative venture where local groups of Native and Non-Native people can collectively identify issues that affect them and take action on resolving the difficulties they face.

We recognize that in order to initiate some kind of action people who commit themselves to a belief must share of their energies and resources. These beliefs are:

1. A recognition of the dignity and self-worth of all Native People in Canada.

2. A recognition of the special status of the Native People of Canada as the original inhabitants of the land.

3. A need to respect the traditions, values and customs of Canada's Original People and to respect their spiritual beliefs.

4. A recognition of the role of Native People as the protectors of the land provided by the Creator.

5. A need to achieve a better understanding between Native and Non-Native People.

6. Through this increased understanding to address ourselves to negative attitudes and actions that show a total disregard for the dignity and self-worth of Canada's Native people.

Issues needed to be addressed can be identified in three categories:

A. Land Claims and Resource development: the development of the North and the search for resources at the expense of the environment and the rights of the Native People who live there.

B. Constitutional Rights: discriminatory practices in Canada towards Native People and their special status in society including the erosion of that status through fragmentation between status, non-status, Metis, etc.

C. Urbanization: the displacement of Native People from their traditional land base thereby forcing them into urban areas.

D. Indian Control of Indian Education

E. Self-Determination.

STATEMENT OF PURPOSE

The Canadian Association in Support of Native Peoples pledges itself to devote its time, energy and resources towards developing local groups of people who will co-operatively study ways and means to achieve a better understanding between Native and Non-Native Canadians and develop plans of action that will help to balance the inequities that exist between the general society and Native people, and begin to show respect and honour for the traditions of Canada's Native people and the environment which has been their home as placed in their care by the Creator.

The Canadian Association in Support of Native Peoples will be, therefore, a voluntary Association of people with the intention:

1. to identify and publicize Canadian concerns that especially affect Native people.

2. specifically to inform Canadian people through relevant organizations and political leaders about these concerns.

3. to rally the support of the Canadian community for response to these concerns by means of daily conversation, cell study and letters to government leaders, to church and community groups and to the news media.

4. to raise money to assist in resolution of such issues as may be dealt with in this way.

5. to maintain coherence in the alliance through a monthly personal financial contribution.

6. to organize simply in order to co-ordinate and sustain this effort.

7. to co-operate with other like-minded organizations.

8. to discover and appoint in every strategic community, key people who will act as instigators of study and action on behalf of the concern mentioned above.

CANADIAN ASSOCIATION IN SUPPORT OF NATIVE PEOPLE: Winnipeg, Manitoba

WHAT WE SAY WE ARE

November 19, 1979

We are the people of the earth
We are in a war that is not of our choosing.
All that we ask is to be allowed to live in peace,
To search out and fulfill the destiny that was intended
For us by the great mystery, the Creator of all that is.
He set us down here on this Great Turtle Island,
This paradise, to walk in a sacred way
And to be the keepers and the custodians
Of this land.
We were to keep the ceremonies and the sacred ways
That He taught us so that we could walk in reverence
And in honour and pass all these things on intact
To the ones who come after us.
We were the keepers of the land when we were
Put here by the great mystery.
That was our bond and we cannot change it
Without His permission, and He has not given His permission.
That is why we the Original People
Must be prepared to give our lives
In defence of our Mother Earth and Her children, the people of the Earth.
This is the final assault by the
Multi-national corporations and their captive state governments.
They have planned and they will execute the final rip-off
Of the Earth's resources
On the pretext of the desperate needs of
The people of today.
And they will leave the children of today and tomorrow
Destitute forever.
There will be no future unless this suicidal race
To destruction is stopped.
And how can it be stopped?
Two ways.

1.

The great mystery will take back possession of this Creation
Again because those who came here from across
The ocean have shown that they have no right to
The stewardship of this land because they have been
Following the ways of the great deceiver,
That great Negative Power.
And unless they are stopped very soon they will make
This Earth uninhabitable for all living things.
Those who love peace do not make bombs
And machines of war.
And it was said that "By their fruits you will know them."

It is evident that the great Negative Power has control
Of the hearts and minds of the vast majority
        of the people of this world
And they in their mindless greed are co-destroyers
With him.
It is also evident that a
Great number of the those people seem not to be
Aware of how they, by their lifestyles, are bringing on
The end of this civilization.
And it is here in the Western Hemisphere that the knowledge
Still remains intact
Of how we are to walk in peace and harmony
With the Creation,
That knowledge was here
before the strangers came and it is here still.

2.

It is obvious to us who try to follow the
Sacred ways that the destruction of the Earth
Is accomplished by human hands and human minds.
And it is also obvious that we will either willingly,
Or mindlessly be a part of that destruction
Or we will set our hearts and minds against it.

POWER IS GIVEN

Power is given to each of us by the Creator.
It is given that we may each accomplish
Our destiny, because there is a purpose for each
Human life.

The notion that we are powerless
Comes from the myths and the lies of that
Monolithic society that lives off the misery
And the anguish of uncounted millions who live
In their jails and in starvation.

The other power that we in the American Indian
Movement recognize is the power of the law.
The power of the law derives from the power
Of the gun and for that reason there can be no
Justice for the Original People of this land.
For a Government that determines to steal
From the Original People
Cannot at the same time give them Justice
Nobody can walk on two roads,
It has to be one or the other,
And on this understanding do we offer our lives
To the Creator for our sacred Mother Earth
And for the People
It is a David and Goliath choice, but if we
Must stand alone, then let it be that way,
but we will always stand tall and strong
Till the last one,
Knowing that the evil power can only
Lose in the end
And there will be peace and harmony on the earth again
And the only laws that remain will be God's laws.

We who walk in this way
Have a strong and clear vision
of how things are
And how they got that way
And where they are going.
We had asked and pleaded for many lifetimes
"Stop destroying the Earth",
But no one would listen.

So now we know
That we must prepare ourselves
For what the prophecies told us so long ago, and
Still tell us today.
That those who destroy Creation
Will in their turn be destroyed
And so we have invested our lives
On the side of the Creator
And ask for His guidance and His blessing
And His protection
Knowing that we can't get out of this
World alive anyway.
So we have no better way than to follow
This vision until it is our time
To return to the Spirit World
From where we came.

All my relations.

WHERE IT WAS

The Indian Eskimo Association:
It seems so long ago that it started out
With a vision of how so many things were wrong
In the Indian World of Kanada,
And with the conviction that concerned and aware
People could be a strong and effective help
Towards justice and common decency.
So they joined hands and hearts and minds
With Native people who were concerned
About the mess they were in
And together they created a monument
To justice and charity, that charity that is love,
And human kindness
In this land.

the time came when Native political
Organizations were formed across the land
And the Indian Eskimo Association
Looked bakc
To the beginning.
And they said, "*Is this the time?*"
For they remembered
They had said,
"When we are no longer needed, we will
Vote ourselves out of existence,"
Is this the time?
And the new leaders said,
"No, we need your help, so stand by."
So the I.E.A. changed its name to
The Canadian Association in Support of Native People
C.A.S.N.P.
And time moved on,
And CASNP found it no longer had
A reason for being,
But it had a lot of things
And a staggering debt.
And at that point
The directors said, "We must seek
A new vision or disappear from the land."

So new directors were chosen in Winnipeg
To pick up the burden
And search
For that new vision.

The New Vision that I see is of people who care about the quality
Of life *for all people* here on this earth.
They talk about Third World or Fourth World
Or underdeveloped people,
But they don't tell you that those people are underdeveloped
And in poverty and despair because the money system
And the military is used
To steal everything they have to that people
In Amerika and Europe can live off the fat
Of the earth while millions starve and live
In conditions that not even animals should be forced to live in.
Surely there will be a time of accounting,
And it is very near,
And surely there are many who would like to help
If only they knew how, even at this late hour.
To those who want to help I can only say this.
You are the only one who can best decide how you should
Invest your time and your energy,
That is between you and the
Great Mystery to decide
No one else.
If you don't like it that way
I can only refer you to what Stokley Carmichael
Said at a meeting in support of the Warriors at
        Wounded Knee, South Dakota.
He said "What it is, is what it is,
It ain't what we like, and it ain't what we want,
It is what it is."

To those who ask how and when or where,
I would say there are so many ways and so many places
And so many opportunities
That I can only tell you this story.
There was a man working on high steel
Who made a mistake and fell off,
He landed on a pile of scrap iron and broken concrete,
Virtually every bone in his body was broken
But he was still alive and still conscious

When they brought him in,
Someone asked him the question,
"Where does it hurt the most?"

At the opening of a "Half-Way House" in Sudbury

COMMITMENT TO SURVIVAL

This house that we call
The New Start Centre
started from a dream
it was a dream that said
"Somehow we must find a way"
to help our brothers and sisters
in the prisons.
We must help them to come out,
and we must make a place where
they can put their lives
back together, a place that will
be good for each one who comes here.

That good way is what we call
Nishnabe Audzaywin.
It means a whole way
of seeing, and being, and believing,
it was the way of our people
for thousands of years in the past.

We have chosen to follow that dream
and that is why the Burwash Native People's Project
came to be what it is.
We say it is a place for healing,
that's what the dream said

That dream lives in our hearts
and it will live on beyond us.
To make this dream happen
took a lot of determination
and commitment.
That it why we require
A Commitment to Survival
from each Sister or Brother
who comes to this place
in search of help,

and the help we give will be on our terms.

A commitment to survival
has to be clearly understood
and agreed to – a signed contract,
before anyone is accepted
into this New Start Centre.

WHY WE ARE HERE

March 14, 1980

Wilderness Camps

Perhaps these camps should be called spiritual wilderness camps
with the emphasis on the spiritual part,
because if we are going to succeed with this work
then it has to be with spiritual power.
They must involve themselves with the power of positive living,
They must teach the elements of positive-negative forces
by which we are dominated.

The leaders must generate as much positive power as possible
starting from the first communal meal,
so as to make the predominant mode in that community of people positive.

Positive equates with spiritual

Negative equates with evil

unless great effort is used right at the beginning
to teach about, and differentiate between, the positive and the negative elements,
there is great danger that the negative will predominate
and if it does then it is only a matter of time
till the whole work will become a negative thing,, which means failure.

So from the first day,
the first morning
it must begin with the sweet grass, the sacred pipe, and the sweat lodge.
it must begin and it must maintain "a praying way".
the reason we must establish the positive element so quickly is because we are now
so totally trained and so totally immersed in the negative way
from the time we are born that it constitutes a total environment for us
just the same as the air totally surrounds us.

It is not that people are bad,
but that we have collectively so many negative ways about us.
Ways of thinking and doing and speaking

If we allow the negative to predominate
such as selfishness,
bad language,
lack of respect for each other, dirty jokes, etc.
then our sense of well being will quickly become unbalanced,
and against our will
we will be forced to begin trying to discipline each other.
From that will come bad feelings,

which in that setting is almost guaranteed to be disastrous.

Discipline

The ideal, and the way it once used to be
even when I was young,
was that we had enough self-discipline
and a strong sense of mutual dependence.
That we governed ourselves according to these principles.
But our young people, coming from a totally artificial environment,
do not understand those two vital principles
because except for rare exceptions
they never had the chance to learn them.

In addition there is one vital principle
that must be acquired for successful "bush living"
and that is self sufficiency,
learning all of the things necessary for survival.
This third principle is something that is acquired
over time and with help from others.

The Indian Way

In this work, we should begin and maintain what we call the Indian Way,
so that in correcting, or teaching, or being corrected
we will always maintain an attitude of respect for each other
or what I call a "gentle" way.

Children

We must have children with us, we need them,
but in that there is a lot of danger too because
more often than not they have learned all sorts of bad ways
of doing in order to attract attention to themselves.
They often become very obnoxious and impossible to deal
with except in very harsh ways.

Just one such child among 20 people
can turn everything sour for everyone
and set people against each other.
That alone can destroy everything for us.
If the mother or the parents can't or won't
bring the child under reasonable control
then others will be forced to
and it's at that point where it can all come apart,

or at least generate very bad feelings
which are very hard to get over,
that is one of the reasons that there should be what I call an "inner council".

An Inner or First Council

There should be a council of four people, *the sacred number*,
At least one or more should be a woman.
Their primary work would be the well being and good order of the camp.
They must have absolute power so that
if necessary they can banish anyone from that camp
who prove by their actions that they will destroy the cohesion
and the good order that everyone is trying to put together.
This is not an elected council.

And the reason that there must be such a council is
that an overall discipline is absolutely essential to success
and if it happens that someone will not or cannot
apply self-discipline then that council would have to act in an appropriate way.
Their meetings would not be open to anyone unless they choose.

People who cannot or will not apply self-discipline
for the good of everyone in the camp
should eliminate themselves from that place immediately.

It may be too, that there should be an overall council
where everyone could have full participation and equal rights
with every other person in the camp
so they could have a full say about whatever is important to them.
That would be the true Indian Way.

It should be the work of such a camp to radicalize the young people:
to make them aware of what is really going on in the cities and towns
and how they must become aware of their power
and how to use it to effect change for the better.
For if we don't want others to continue to determine our destiny,
then we must take a firm hold of the present
and make the future what we want it to be.
That is what self determination is all about.

We should think of using resources such as books and written materials
for teaching,
and we should perhaps have some time set aside each day
to teach in an organized way, like maybe an hour a day for compulsory teaching.
But if there is to be a time for compulsory teaching
the "students" should have a full say in it.

There should also be an opportunity for a craft programme:
wood carving, tanning hides, making moccasins and such things,
but on a casual basis.

The primary goal of such a wilderness camp is to learn
how to live in harmony with Creation.
That means with the trees and the plants and all living things.
Our first consideration is to get ourselves *in balance.*
that is, we must get ourselves happy and contented
and anyone who upsets that balance for us is doing wrong,
so we must be careful to try to get ourselves in that way
and not to knowingly or deliberately upset someone else.

I suppose it means to learn to walk on the earth in a sacred way,
with respect for each other
because that brings peace and good order.
If we go about it in that way, "the positive way",
there's little danger that things can go wrong
and we should be the happiest people you have ever seen.
always happy, always laughing and caring about each other.

I'm not saying that all of us will get along first class together,
because there are always some of us who will give out
the wrong vibrations for someone else.
That is always a fact of life, so it is well to keep some distance between us,
so that we do not interfere with each other.

Living Space

It is natural and normal that a couple or a family
should disagree among themselves and for that reason
they should be able to be a little ways apart from others
so that they can work out their disagreements in private
without everyone knowing all the details of their private lives.
So every couple should have the right and the opportunity
to live separately as it suits their needs, in tents or teepees.

Tension

I say that in every community there is tension,
"something which holds them *together.*"

That tension can be cohesive or destructive.
It might be called the politics of the village.
There are many forces that operate.
That tension can be positive or negative.

If it is positive it is the "glue" that holds them together.
If it is negative it is the power that divides them.
If it becomes powerful enough it can simply disintegrate that community of people.
Again I want to tell you: Positive equals good or spiritual.
negative equals evil.

This is why it is so essential to build that positive power
as fast as possible
so that as the negativism begins to show, it is overwhelmed.
This positive-negative is sort of invisible
but those are the dynamics that underlie
all community living.

If you went to many small communities you would see
that each village has a character all its own
and that it is made up of negative and positive elements
in that community, people and ideas.

Interdependence

One of the essentials of good community living is that people
mutually recognize their interdependence with each other.
That will be one of the hardest things to teach our young people.
In fact almost anyone who comes
from the totally artificial environment of city-living
will find it hard to learn
because it is essential to balance interdependence
with individual independence and self sufficiency.
It is absolutely essential for everyone to be independent
so as to maintain their own individuality
and a strong regard for their own unique personality or self,
but the force that operates to teach people that essential element is, like in times of
great danger from the elements, in need of limiting.
It is in times of great danger
that people come to realize how much they need each other
and it is then that they learn how to interact so as to be mutually supportive.

Mutually Supportive

That is the key. That is what made it all possible for our people to live
so well with an environment that was sometimes deadly for the unwary.

Being mutually supportive doesn't mean you have to like everybody around you.
That is sometimes impossible.
It does mean that when the crunch comes you'll put your life
on the line for your brother or sister
if that's how it has to be,
and likes or dislikes have nothing to do with it.
That's the kind of guarantee we need from each other.

Radios

There should be no radios in a wilderness camp.
They are "mind benders", they distort reality.
There should be no radio in the camp unless it is considered essential by the Inner
Council.

Care of Food, Clothing and Equipment

It seems to be extremely hard to make our young people understand
that having a thoughtful and deliberate regard
for the care of food, clothing and equipment
will be directly related to their ability to survive into the very near future.
If they are going to persist in defying the first rule of survival
they will almost guarantee that nobody it going to make it, when we will need every
scrap of food and clothes and other essential things
during the time of purification.

It is not the Indian Way to be destructive and
to disregard the ordinary rules of common sense.
That is a fool's way.
In that sense I too have loaned various things to others such as
a feather blanket, boots, canoes, canvas, tools, and many other things.
Often they have been loaned to others
with complete disregard for my rights as a person,
never bothering to ask if it's ok with me or not,
so that the things which I have so diligently provided myself with,
to guarantee my own survival and the survival of others,
literally becomes common property
and I have to forcibly intervene
in order to have any say in the matter.
That sure isn't the "Indian" way.

It is the way of disruption and disorder.

We should remember that it is one of the first misconceptions
that the "hippies" had.
They seemed to take it for granted that all property was communal property
and that no one should be unhappy if his personal possessions
belonged equally to everyone else.
That was one of the prime reasons why they could never keep it together.

That business of people borrowing from me
and then lending in turn to others
without ever asking me if it's all right is a troublesome question.
It leaves me with only two alternatives: 1) be stingy, or 2) own nothing.

If I own nothing I will be extremely upset because
there is no way I can provide for myself let alone others,
and if I become stingy I couldn't live with myself let alone others.
In all the years I have lived I have yet to see "common property" taken care of
unless police are set up to guard it and, as you know,
Indian people never had police.
What Indian people did have was personal possessions
that were regarded as sacred to that person alone
and that only unusual circumstance changed that law of the people.

I can remember many unusual circumstances
in my lifetime of bush living when it was necessary to break into someone's shack
in the bush and use the food and things we found there
but we took great care to inform the owner as soon as it was possible
and to restore or replace anything necessary
in order to get things in a good way again.
Those were often life and death matters
and for that reason many of us never put a lock on a door
so that others would have to break in in a time of need
and it was also for that reason that we always made sure that
there was some food left behind in case someone needed it.

I will give you this example about the question of personal belongings
so that you will be aware of one of the ways
that can quickly get us into deep trouble
and perhaps stop what we are trying to do.
This is one more reason why we must only have serious minded people
in these camps.
People who are looking for fun and games should go somewhere else
or stay where they are at.

The Psychology of Survival

It is because we are dealing first with attitudes of the mind and heart
and who we are
and what is the part that the Creator gave to us
so that we could be part of His ongoing Creation.
It is because of these things that we should consider
that our first work is the psychology of survival,
and the second is survival itself
although in practice these things are not divided.
Our essential work is to put ourselves back together
as it used to be, a spiritual people living in a whole way again.

A whole way by definition means a Holy Way

I suppose it sounds kind of solemn and serious
but it reminds me of a guy who was drowning off a dock in New York City.
He was yelling, "Help, Help! I can't swim"
and the fat guy standing on the dock yelled back,
"I can't swim either, but would ten dollars help you?"

A Vision of Renewal & Rehabilitation

There is a sacred principle or commandment;
"Thou shalt love thy neighbour as thyself."

This was given as a sacred principle or instruction to live by,
Not as words to be hidden away in a book;
that if the sacred principle were totally accepted and lived by
There could be no such things as prisons.

The reality is that there are prisons; and that a high percentage
Of inmates are Native people,
We who have visited those inmates for some years have been made aware,
by those inmates that some of them could come out on parole,
Often years before their full sentence is served;
If only they had a place to which they might go.

We also believe that many young people
get into trouble with the
Law and often begin a life of crime because of broken families and
the Lack of care and concern for them
as human beings;
And the lack of training and teaching that would come
from a strong and stable
Family that knew from where it came
and what its purpose in life is.

We believe that we are our brothers' keepers

And that some day each of us will be called back to the spirit world
That we came from, when each of us will have to answer the same question:

> *"what have you done*
> *With the time*
> *And the opportunities*
> *And the gifts*
> *That I gave to you?"*

It is on this basis that our faith is founded.

Are we wrong if we dare to reach out to help others?

From these principles and with this purpose,
we went to both the federal government and the Ontario government
to ask for unused land and buildings at Burwash
so that we might put together a plan and a place of rehabilitation
to bring this vision to reality.

Rehabilitation

We do not propose to make farmers or gardeners out of anyone
but it seems essential that for a sound mind to form,
there needs to be a sound body.
This speaks in large letters:
FOOD and PEACE and TRANQUILITY
and a place to grow emotionally and psychologically
to achieve a balance with the Creation.

The disastrous life-way that Native people have come
To know as "normal" is a totally disrupted way –
spiritually, physically, emotionally, psychologically
And for a vast number of young people
It is directionless and purposeless.
There is virtually no one for them to turn to for help and guidance.

Are we to allow these young ones
to be sacrificed on the altar of greed
Or are they God's children too?

We know the process by which our families came to such disastrous times.

And we know the way back.

We know that the Creator created
The western hemisphere and that He created
The Native people and put them down here
With their original instructions;

He told them that they were to walk in harmony
With the Creation and to be the *keepers of the land*;
Only He could ever be the owner of the land.
We also know that one of the greatest healing powers He gave us was WORK.

And for that reason we propose to teach the meaning
And the sacredness of work.

We also know that the Creator gave to His children
Here in this land, the sacred ways that they were
To follow.
He was the one who gave us the sweat lodge, the sacred
pipe, the sun dance, the sacred drum.
Those sacred ways were His invention
Not the invention of Man,
And if they were pagan ways
Then so is the Inventor of those ways – a pagan.

For the healing rehabilitation to begin
We must re-establish the sacred principles
And put them at the centre –
A guiding light if you will,
Not on the basis of compulsion
But because so many of the Native inmates
Are constantly saying the spiritual concerns are
Their top priority.
And for years now, our young people
Have been searching out and finding the
Medicine people, the spiritual leaders and
the sacred ceremonies to satisfy the
Gnawing hunger that can be satisfied in no other way.

And because we are being given such clear and
Strong directions from those we are trying
To help, we will put the sacred drum,
The sacred pipe, and the sweat lodge,
And the sacred teaching
At the centre of everything we do.
For this we must have the kind of people
who can respect and help these ways to be strong.

There are priests and ministers and people
Of the cloth, who see clearly that these ways
Must come back if the Native people are to become
Strong again, and it will happen that way;
It is happening fast already

And the only people of religion who feel threatened
Are those who are fanatics or are unsure of
Themselves or their beliefs.

Of this I am certain:
In all of Creation there is only
one source of Truth and that is God himself.

And no matter how it is presented
Or where it comes from
There can be no contradiction;
The real truth cannot contradict itself.

Families

If broken families result in so many of our people
Ending up in prison
Then surely a strong element in the rehabilitation
Is to give them the opportunity to participate
In a wholesome family life;
Which means men, women and children must be living and
Working and participating in all the things that are
Being done at Burwash.

Gardening and Self-Sufficiency

The Burwash Native Peoples Project proposes to
Reach the highest degree of self-sufficiency possible.
That is why it proposes to cut wood for community use
and to sell it to others;
Proposes to do some limited farming
And each family would undertake to have their own Family garden –
partly to provide their own food
And partly to acquire knowledge and skills that they
Can take home to their own communities when they leave.
One of the criteria for choosing a family to come and live there
Might be that a member of the family be able to
Teach trapping or craft work or other skills –
In that way there will be a transfer of mutually beneficial
Knowledge and skills

This paper does not undertake to detail all that proposes
To happen at Burwash or some other land
That it might be set down on.
What it does propose to do is

To show the vision of what wants to happen and why it
Must happen, if not at Burwash then at some other place;
And we are looking for that place and the means to do it with.

If any or all of this seems impossible
Just remember that there was a time
When people decided what must be done
And they did it.

It is the principle of self-determination that we must make
Operative again.

The time has come again
A work of healing must now begin
It could begin at Burwash.

CHAPTER EIGHT

Into All the World

The authentic quality of Art's message is reflected in the way that his concern for justice and mercy has grown beyond national or cultural boundaries without losing sight of its point of origin. Art Solomon's words on behalf of his own people in North America have been sought and heard in many lands.

In the 1960's, Art's interest in crafts took him to South America. His justice concerns took him, in 1977, to the World Council of Indigenous People's conference in Switzerland. His inter-faith concerns moved the World Council of Churches to invite him to a conference on the Island of Mauritius in February 1983. In August 1983, he was an observer at the World Council of Churches in Vancouver where he wrote the pieces: *Affirmation*, *The Wheels of Justice*, and *To the Most Sacred*.

The next year, in 1984, he attended the World Council on Religion and Peace Conference in Nairobi where he contributed *A Vision of Life from the Sacred Midewiwin*. In 1988, he attended the World Council on Religion and Peace Conference in Australia.

With the fire of a Biblical prophet, Art speaks to the contemporary Christian churches of judgement and repentance. Although he shows no patience with the prejudice and arrogance of much organized religion, it is not religion that Art condemns, but rather the failure of its nominal adherents to practice what they preach. The insights he brings from aboriginal wisdom give comfort and direction to those who are seeking a more authentic way of living.

Before he will present this message to an institution such as the World Council of Churches, Art says that he waits to see if they are "just going to pull out their theological marbles and play with them", or if they want to struggle with the real issues. The selections in this chapter are evidence that there is real struggle going on, and that Art's powerful message is being heard.

Art's work in the larger world is not confined to major institutions. He has given guidance and counsel to many individuals who find in his teachings the principles they can use to build a new life.

– m.p.

Written for the World Council of Churches on the Island of Mauritius

GRANDFATHER LOOK AT OUR BROKENNESS

Grandfather
Look at
Our brokenness
Now we must put
The sanctity of Life
As the most sacred principle
Of power,
And renounce
The awesome might
Of materialism.
We know that in all Creation
Only the family of man
Has strayed,
From the sacred way.

We know that we are the ones
Who are divided
And we are the ones
Who must come back,
Together,
To worship and walk
In a sacred way,
That by
Our affirmation,
We must heal the earth
And heal each other.

To the World Conference on Indigenous People, Geneva Switzerland

To Friends
Whoever They Are
And Wherever They May Be.

October 10, 1977
Garson, Ontario, Canada

This letter is written in response to my need to give a report to those who sent me to the World Council at Geneva, September 20-23, 1977. It is also written for those three people who dug deep into their pockets to buy tickets and provide the money for hotels and meals, out of their own sense of commitment to the human family. It is also written for those many people in different countries who will receive copies of the final documents that came from that Conference. They are not documents of words, they are documents of action, in the words of Romesh Chandra, Chairman of the Subcommittee: "We end this conference with a clear cut declaration of solidarity with Indigenous Nations and Peoples. We have not finished something. We are now going to begin action on a world scale."

My personal feeling about the conference was that it was a total success when I think of the dynamics involved, and I mean in terms of the international power politics and the internal conflicts that we have among ourselves as Native People, it would have to be a miracle for us to succeed so well with such a work. The days before the conference began we came very close to a major explosion among the Native Leadership. The morning of the conference we all came together and the oldest warrior said a prayer in the Old Hopi Way with the Sacred Corn. From there we followed the drum for three-quarters of a mile to the *Palais des Nations*, three warriors walked in front with the Sacred Pipe to the conference table, the only songs were sung by the warriors who carried the Sacred Drum. One was the A.I.M. Song which is the Native People's Flag Song or National Anthem. The second was the Chief's Song which was sung in honour of those who were to speak on behalf of the Native Nations. Those songs can truly be described as prayers.

The first words at the conference were a prayer to the Creator with the Sacred Pipe. And during the whole conference, each morning before sunrise people were praying with the Sacred Pipe and in Canada and the USA our people were also praying with the Sacred Pipe and praying with the Sacred Tobacco.

We went to that conference and we delivered a total message, a complete package, and despite our differences it was accomplished in total unity, it was a miracle accomplished before our eyes.

From my point of view we went to Geneva to deliver a message to the world about how it is with us, the Native People here in America. We delivered that message and the world heard very clearly what we said, and those who heard understand that they must now act.

I would be troubled if my trust depended only on men and women in the context of the message that we brought to Geneva. But the way I see it, there is the precise timing of the Creator in this work, it's as if the Native Nations have gone halfway around the world to go and pray to God in that place up in the mountains and He said: "My children I have heard your prayers. I have seen your suffering, and I will dry your tears."

These words may seem foolish to some because they speak so strongly about the spiritual aspects of the conference, but to me the whole thing was a spiritual exercise, and in a limited way it was a triumph of Good over Evil.

I think it is true to say that together in solidarity, we the oppressed and the wretched of the Earth along with a multitude of the human family, have reached out our hands across the oceans and the continents of the world to become of one mind in action and in prayer, and together we will take the measure of the monster that oppresses us and of those governments that facilitate that evil work. What we want is peace and good order on the Earth so that the human family can search again for the Creator's vision of how we were to walk about in a Sacred Way here in this world, for we are only visitors here for a short time. For these Blessings, Grandfather, great Spirit, we give thanks. Kitche Megwitch.

Art Solomon
Delegate
Spiritual Advisor,
American Indian Movement,
Canada.

LETTER TO SWEDEN

Svensk-Indianska Forbundet
c/o Britt-Marie Johansson
Malmo, Sweden

Dear friends:

I give thanks to the Creation that you wrote to me concerning the nuclear power development in your country.

Here in Ontario they also are developing nuclear power to generate electricity and some of the people are aware of the great danger that it means *to all living things*, but there are a great many people who are either sleeping or they wish to continue to live in their fool's paradise.

That's what it is – *a fool's paradise* – but their dreams will shortly turn into the horrible nightmare that they really are and there will be no one to comfort them because nuclear power is God's creation and we were never to have played with it as if it were our own.

If nuclear power were left in the ground where it was supposed to be then everything about it would remain in balance.

But some people – the military-industrial complex, wanted more effective weapons to kill people, it doesn't matter whether they are capitalists or communists.

They follow the Great Negative Power, he is their leader.

That's where it's at in this world: the two greatest powers are the positive and the negative;

The Creator is the great positive power – all of this Creation is His;

We breathe the air; we drink the water that He made for use;

We walk among His trees and plants; they are our food and our medicines;

The four winds and the great seas belong to Him;

All the children of the earth are His children;

They are of four colours; we call them four sacred colours;

They are black, yellow, red and white; all equally precious to Him;

And none were to have power over others;

We were created equal with equal rights and responsibilities, and when we return to the spirit world where we came form, there will be no racism and hatred and no greed. All of the Creation follows their original instructions; the animals, the birds, the fish and the plants...the four great winds and the waters, everything in the Creation except the family of man.

But there are those who work hard to convince us that *we need nuclear power*. They succeed to convince a great number who either choose to live mindlessly or have no alternative but to continue destroying the earth that we live on. But we must remember that this is still God's Creation and He is very much in control every minute of the night and day and He will not allow fools to destroy His work. He will destroy them first, He *must*, or nothing can live here.

There are only two ways, either we walk in peace and harmony or we are destroyers of the earth, and those who destroy will be destroyed – there is no other way. So we have a responsibility for what we do with our hearts and minds because we will all be asked the same question:

"What have you done with the time and the opportunities and the gifts that I gave to you?"

If we follow those who choose to develop this nuclear insanity then we are writing our own death certificate and while we are still living we are attending our own funeral and the funerals of our own children and the faces of countless others who are still "coming towards us" will be turned back because we have fixed it so that there is no place on the earth for them to live.

All I am saying is that we must be sure of the direction we are choosing to follow. If we choose to follow fools then let it be so; but we must be prepared to accept the results of our decision. We have one prime responsibility: We must not deceive others and above all we must not deceive ourselves.

It was a Mohawk woman who said to the president and the people of the USA:

'When you have cut down the last tree
And when you have killed the last fish
And when you have destroyed the last river,
It is then that you will understand
That you cannot eat all the gold
That you have put in the bank.''

These are my words.

Art Solomon
Spiritual advisor
American Indian Movement

GREAT PRAYER

To the most sacred and profound mystery,
the Creator of the Universe and of
humankind, I send these thought
and these prayers.

August 1983
Vancouver, British Columbia

I give thanks
    For the power
        And the beauty
        And the sacredness
        Of your Creation.
I give thanks
    For the spirit helpers
        Who come to help
        And who inspire us
        With wisdom and understanding
        From the world beyond.
I send these thoughts to you
    The Creator and the keeper
        Of the universe.
        I send these words of affirmation and hope.
For all that lives
    here on Earth Mother
        How could it be
        That you the Holy One,
        The supreme architect, the maker and the keeper
        Of all life,
        How could it be that you would let your work be destroyed
        By the hand of man?
        Was that part of your plan?

No.
    The scales are balanced
        Beyond the vision of man;
        The measures of good and evil
        That only you can see.

No.
    Your work will not be destroyed
        By the hand of man
        For you are God, the positive power
        And the negative one will not prevail
        Because this is the final test,
        And the negative can not win.

I send this prayer
    And these words of affirmation
        To you my sisters and brothers
        Who stand and fight
        This negative power
        By your prayers and thoughts
        And positive actions.

Have courage.
    Stand tall and strong
        And never give up the fight;
        Because the one who stands with you is God.
        The one who gave you life
        And who asks only that you stand firm
        Against all evil no matter how violent.
        This year of God,
        It's number one thousand nine hundred and eighty three,
        This is the year of turning
        Before our eyes
        The negative will diminish
        And the positive will grow.

We do not need weapons of holocaust
    To make the world safe for humans.
        We need hearts and minds of love and clear determination
        So all that lives will have a future
        Beyond this time of terror.

To you the churches and
    Faith traditions
        I give this challenge.
If the word of God is real
    When He said:
        "You shall love thy neighbour..."
        Then show me.
        Don't tell me
        Because I have no more time to listen.
I say to you: *"Get real or get lost."*
    If you lived by only one commandment,
        "Love thy neighbour . . .,"
        Then the prisons would be empty
        And there could be peace on earth.
SHOW ME . . .

30 SECONDS TO MIDNIGHT

I find myself in a strange situation here today because my major thrust in life is not economic development but whether life will continue on this planet or not. Perhaps those who plan and hope for economic development have a lot more faith than I have.

This summer the most important statement that was made by the World Council of Churches in their final documents was, "If there is no justice, there will be no peace on earth," spoken by Dr. Alan Boesak. Therefore the World Council of Churches must come down on the side of people who are engaged in Liberation struggles all over the earth and must join in those struggles for justice.

The alternative is a nuclear holocaust and if that happens the story is ended anyway.

The youth component of W.C.C. at the Sixth Assembly this year spoke in great anger. They said "You call us 'the church of the Future', but we are people *Who Do Not Look To A Future*. For that reason we demand that you hear us now."

It is in this context that we consider the question of economic development by Native people in this country today. I am very uncomfortable, and I propose to share with you the nature of my discomfort, but I'm not sure that I can do it in five minutes.

I have been involved in a liberation struggle in this land all my life, and as long as I live in this body that I walk around in I will stand with those in struggle until I see all the birds flying backwards. I respect the rights of others to follow their own vision in the process of their liberation and I expect the same in return. I have no criticism to offer to those who propose to make economic development happen *for* and *with* Native people, but I have some experience and some very strong thoughts about it.

We as Native people have had the experience of so many other oppressed indigenous people around the world: the experience of having been culturally, economically, and spiritually devastated by those who called themselves Christian and Civilized. In their great kindness they have designated us among the people of the Third World.

It's at this time in history of the human family that we find ourselves adopting various means to accomplish our liberation.

Liberation is not only a necessity, it is an imperative. We are God's children and it seems to me that God never intended that any of His children should be oppressed and denied their right to live and share in His abundance. He gave us life to celebrate not to endure. We have been denied the right to our inheritance by the treachery, and the greed, and the manipulation of others.

But this is a new day and the ways of greed must give place to the ways of need. If that is not so then this is not God's world and He has gone away and left us. But God has not gone away, and He has not forgotten about us. We are still just as precious to Him as any of His children.

From this point I begin to share my discomfort. I have to ask, what is the point of getting on a bus that ain't going nowhere? In other words the money will die, so what then?

The question for me is not about money, but what about us? What are we going to do when this present system comes into total chaos. Will we know how to take care of ourselves and of each other as we once did?

I say that we have withstood the onslaught of Christianity and Civilization and we are still here, and I say that if the earth will survive so will we, the people of the earth survive, but it will not be with money NO it will be because we have learned how to live in harmony with God's Creation again. And I also say that those who destroy God's Creation will be destroyed by its power.

I don't think the sun and the moon and the Creation around us has lost any of its power. Maybe we should look again at those things and think about what they mean to us.

We were once called savages and worshippers of evil spirits but no people in the history of the human family have so savaged the earth as those who presently walk on this sacred land and call themselves civilized and enlightened.

According to Dr. Gillian Baker of New York city, there were nine previous empires before this present one, and all of them followed precisely the same pattern. As though in lock-step down through the centuries, she said each of them came to their highest point of arrogance, and from there went downhill fast, to their oblivion. They are not around any more. And she said to the U.S.A. that their highest point of arrogance was when they destroyed the cities of Hiroshima and Nagasaki in a most incredible waste of human life.

It was said of the Roman Empire when it was disintegrating that they gave the peoples cakes and circuses, presumably to distract them from the reality.

But the Empire fell. It is gone, and so will this present empire fall, just as sure as the sun will come up tomorrow.

The circuses we already have in the capital cities of this country, but this money that has been designated, for Indian Economic Development, is that the cakes and the cookies and the goodies to distract us from reality?

In my mind the reality that governments have in mind for the Native people of Canada is to separate them once and all from the land and the resources, in the words of the 1969 white paper policy, they said they were "going to make us *equal*". We understood very clearly what kind of equality they meant by that policy that's why we opposed it so strongly all across this land.

Now the government in Ottawa has patriated the constitution and they mean to do precisely what they were prevented from doing in 1969.

In the words of George Manuel, they will negotiate with the Native leaders in Ottawa for four years, then they will tell us exactly what rights we have, that is precisely why the word "existing" was inserted, before it was presented to the British parliament. And like Pontius Pilate, the British parliament washed their hands and absolved themselves of their responsibility.

Now its "made in Canada" all the way, and I would remind you that the unwritten, consistent policy of the Governments of Canada has always been "The Disappearing Indian". That was and still is the prime responsibility of the department of Indian Affairs in Canada.

Part of the ongoing plan has been to put some millions of dollars on the table for native Economic Development.

Bait. That's what it is, bait.

We are still the protectors of this land and we will be asked to account for that responsibility by the only One who has the right to claim ownership of this planet and its resources.

It makes little difference who destroys and depletes the resources of this land and the results are always the same. People seem to forget that they belong not only to us but to future generation as well, we should not be deluded by present technology. Present technology is making sure that there will be no future inheritance for anybody, we have only to look in the faces and listen to the words of the young people of today.

The technology is devised and applied by the military and the multi-national corporations of the world. Governments are the *captives* of those corporations.

Progress and development are the magic words, the results are death and destruction. I call it a fools paradise where people believe that they have a right to live off the inheritance of other human beings and to steal the inheritance of the unborn and still believe they are sane and civilized people, what a pity.

I am not saying don't take their money. What I am saying is, first look into your hearts and look into the wisdom of those who went before us and with the wisdom of those who walk on this land now ask, "What Is The Price?"

The old ones said long ago, that "When we make decisions we have to think of seven generations into the future, because what we decide now will affect them when they come to this world."

A wise man once said, "The people will always know what to do provided they have the context in which to do it." Will you try to provide that context?

I know one department of government who have always made sure that such a context never existed in any real way for Native people, but that is the nature of parasites.

One of my greatest concerns is, as a wise Indian leader said, here in September, that money could end up in the hands of *The Fat Cat Indians* and the people will get nothing. If you can help the process of human development for the original people of Canada. I'm all for it.

Kitchi Meegwetch.

From the Sacred Mideiwin way (mid-day-win) of the Ojibwa Nation

SHARING A VISION OF LIFE

August 1984
Nairobi, Kenya

My sisters and my brothers of the world community
    I give thanks that I can be a part of the work that you
        are doing to bring peace and tranquillity to a troubled world.

If in what I say you hear the screams of my people in their
    distress please forgive me,
        because it has been a daily experience
        for nearly 500 years.

The spiritual ways of our people were outlawed
    and driven underground for a long time
        but now they are coming back again,
        they are coming back because they must.

The sacred ways of our people were given to us
    by the Creator and brought to us by the spirit helpers.

We recognize the Creator in His Creation
    And for that reason everything
        that has been created is sacred;
        The fire, and the water, and the air that we breath
        are sacred;
        The plants and the animals, the birds and the fish
        are sacred;
        They were here on the sacred mother earth
        before there was human life.
        They were able to get along very well without us
        but we cannot live without them.
        So we constantly give thanks that they support our lives.

We look in the sky and we see our elder brother sun
    and we give thanks that he is still following
        His original instructions.
        We know that without Him there would be no life
        on this earth.

We look again in the sky and see our grandmother moon
    and the star world
        and we know that our grandmother moon is still doing
        her work to look after all the female life on the earth;
        her work is to take care of all the fertility of all female life.

We know that all the medicine to cure
    human sickness was put in the plants
        and when we want medicine for our sicknesses
        we have to talk to the plants and give them sacred
        tobacco and explain why we have to take their lives
        for our healing, or for our food.
        If we take the lives of animals or birds or fish
        to support our lives we have to give thanks to them;
        If we travel on water or use water to keep life
        in our bodies we give thanks to the water
        because it is life;
        Nothing can live without it.

We give thanks for the gift of fire
    because it is sacred;
        It was said that when you offer your tobacco to the fire
        "I will see your prayers in the smoke."
        We give thanks to all of the Creation in that way,
        It is said that tobacco is one of the sacred elements:
        the sacred tobacco, the sage, the cedar
        and the sacred sweet grass;
        these were given for us to pray with.
        When we pray this way we say to our people that we
        clean ourselves with this sacred smoke
        so that for this short time that we are praying
        it is to bring our hearts and minds together as one
        to eliminate all negative thoughts from
        our hearts and minds while we pray.

In our way of praying we are more concerned to give
    thanks for so much that it is given to us
        rather than to ask for more, because everything
        is given to us freely for our needs;
        We pray always for our sisters and brothers and our relations
        rather than for ourselves
        except to pray for guidance and blessing and protection
        so that we can walk in a good way.

This morning I have first washed myself with the smoke
of the sacred things.
Then I offered them to you for a blessing
and then I give thanks to the four sacred medicine
Grandfathers,
to our Earth Mother
and to plant life, and the animal life and the bird life
and the fish life.
I offer the sacred incense to the fire and the water
and to our elder brother the sun
and to our Grandmother Moon and the sky world
and to the thunder people who bring the rain
to give life to all things.

Then I offer the sacred smoke to the spirit helpers
and to my spirit helpers
and to the great mystery, the Creator of all things.

There are many sacred ceremonies that we have,
like the Sundance and the Sweat Lodge
and there are many sacred songs that are given
to some of our people by the spirit helpers.

I would like to share with you the story of the sacred pipe.
The stone bowl represents all the female life in the Creation
and the stem that is usually made of wood represents all the
male life in the Creation;
together they are complete.
When we pray with the sacred pipe we offer tobacco
to the four sacred medicine powers,
to the Earth Mother, to the spirit beings,
and we ask them to sit with us and smoke with us.
We recognize that we need their help and blessing
and guidance to walk in balance.

The story was told
that one day a spirit being came to a village in the form
of a human being and he told the people
that they were going to be given a new ceremony
to help them in the time ahead.
He explained the ways in which the pipe was to be used
and that it had a lot of power.
It had power to harm as well as to help

and when the pipe was used to make a promise
that promise was never to be broken;
that is how all the treaties in North America
were made and still today none of our people
have ever broken a promise that was made in that way.

The people were told that on a certain day
they were to send out two warriors to a place
that was appointed, two beautiful young men.

They were standing in that place and off in the distance
they could see something white coming towards them,
when it came close they saw that it was a beautiful
young woman carrying a bundle in her arms.
One of those young man had the wrong kind
of thoughts in his mind.
When she came close she turned to give him the
bundle that she carried,
then she said to the other one,
"All right, now you can do what you want,"
As he reached for her a cloud covered them and when the cloud
went away all that was left of that young man was his
bones on the ground.
The young woman turned and walked away and off in the distance
she turned into a white buffalo calf.

The original sacred pipe that was given
from the spirit world is still in America today,
but it was once almost lost to the Bureau of Indian Affairs of USA.
Today, there are many sacred pipes and our people are using them
to pray
for all the Creation, for the earth and the people
who are so much in need of healing.

It is clear to us that all of Creation still follows
its original instructions except the human family
and that is why we are in so much distress,
so out of balance.

Conclusion

I would like to suggest to you that here
        we must begin to weave
                a tapestry of life together;
                each of us has brought a thread that is made
                from our understanding, our hope, our dedication,
                our faith in God, and our love for our fellow human beings.
                As we worked here together during these few days
                each of us has contrived to weave our own thread
                into the fabric of love that we are making here together.
                We need to remember that in Nairobi,
                here in this sacred land, we have only begun the weaving
                and when we go to our homes we must join with
                others who are also weaving their own parts of that
                fabric of life.
                When we have woven them all into one we can cover the whole
                world
                with a blanket of peace and tranquillity
                which derives from love, which is the power of God.

We need perhaps always to remember
        that we are children of God.
                No one less important or less precious than another
                and that life is given for us to celebrate,
                not to endure.
                And here we have truly celebrated life together
                in our prayers, in our laughter,
                in our work, and in our many ways of worship to God.
                Yes, we have celebrated life together here
                in reverence and respect for each other.
                We must walk in that way for as long as we walk on this earth.

When the scientists and the technologists
        leave off from solving the mysteries of God and of life
                and learn instead to have a reverence for His Creation,
                then we will have arrived.
                We need only to know how to walk in peace and tranquillity
                in God's Creation, then we will not have to be concerned.

This is not a dream,
  it is a reality that we can make real for all of us
    if we have the courage, the determination, and the vision
    that we have shared here together.
    The power to do it has already been given to us;
    It is that irresistible, invincible power called Love,
    which is the essence of God.

We must not say or think,
  "I am too small, too insignificant,
    what I do doesn't matter;"
    because each of us is vitally important
    in this final battle with the power of evil,
    my constant prayer to God is to ask
    for that great evil power to be diminished and sent away.

And since each of us is a part of God who created us
  then we have a vital interest in changing the world
    that we live in, so it is vitally important what we do
    with our hearts and our minds.

I would like to share a story with you.
  It is called the prophecy of the seven fires.
    I begins when our people, the Ojibway nation,
    lived by the great salt water, the Atlantic Ocean.
    It told about our migration to the west,
    perhaps over centuries.
    It said there would be seven stopping places called seven fires.
    In each of those places we would establish our sacred fire,
    Our spirit offerings, our thanksgiving for all life.

Our last stopping place would be beside a lake
  Lake Superior.
    It is said also that we would almost lose our sacred way.
    It ends by saying that the people of the seventh fire
    would be the ones who would retrace their steps
    to find *the sacred bundles* that were left behind.
    We have come to see that we are the people who were spoken of,
    The *People of the Seventh Fire*.
    And it is said that if the seventh fire was able
    to light the eighth fire,
    there would be peace on earth for all the Creation.

I would like to say to those who called us pagans and savages,
    that at no time in the history of the human family
        has the earth and the people of the earth been
        so savaged as it is now,
        by those who call themselves Christian and civilized.
        Surely it is not already too late to turn around
        and walk in the way of peace and reverence.
        And I would say to those who still believe that we are pagans:
        "My truth does not invalidate your truth
        and your truth does not invalidate mine."

I say to each of you, do not walk in fear
    but with courage and a clear purpose
        because with the power of God which is already yours
        there's no way else that we can do but win.

Kitche Manitou
    I give thanks for the power and the beauty and the
    sacredness of your Creation.
    This story has no end but this is all that I
    can share with you for this time.

          Ho Mitakwias.

THE WORLD WE LIVE IN

January, 1985

It is God the Creator,
    The great Mystery,
        Who conceived the first thought,
        Who spoke the first word.

It is God who fashioned
    All of the known and the unseen Creation
        In harmony and balance.

It is only a part of the human family
    Which has put *everything out of balance*;
        And it is only a small part
        Of the human family
        Which insists on threatening all life on this planet
        With extinction.

And now in a desperate search for a solution
    To this present insanity
        God seems to be the one who is
        almost entirely left out.

The only one *who has all the answers*
    Is the only one who is almost
        Never asked.

Yet this is still God's world
    And we are His-Her guests;
        Is it not about time we ask,
        What we are doing here in this part
        Of God's Creation?
        Or is it already too late
        To ask the question?

OUR DESTINY IS NOT NEGOTIABLE

Our destiny as descendants
    Of the original people of this land
        Is not negotiable
        With any governments
        At any time
        Or any place
        In any way.

Our destiny, our inheritance, our rights
    And our responsibilities as
        Children of God
        Come from the Great Mystery Himself
        Not from any governments
        However constituted.

We did not cross the Bering strait
    As the anthropologists say.
        Our ancestors
        Were put here by God
        To be the caretakers of this land.
        We were not put here on this earth
        To steal the inheritance
        Of the unborn
        Our covenant, our bond,
        Can only be with our ancestors
        Who kept faith with the Creator's original purpose
        And with those still unborn
        Who will come after us.

Therefore we have no right
    To negotiate the destiny
        Of ourselves or of our children
        Who will come
        To claim their inheritance
        In their own time.

We cannot and we will not
        Negotiate the rights to our future
                With captive state governments
                Who speak and negotiate on behalf of
                Transnational corporations.
                We are not confused nor misled
                About their real intentions.
                We believe that there is enough
                On God's earth for everyone's needs.

And we have no right to abdicate our responsibility
        Or to negotiate the inheritance of God's children
                And sacrifice their rights,
                To the greed
                Of the multinational corporations.
                They call it progress and development.
                We call it death and destruction.

Our rights as human beings
        Come from God not from governments.
                And they are not negotiable.

Among those rights
        Is the right to live unmolested
                And in peace on a land base
                That is adequate to meet the needs
                Of ourselves and our families.

THEY'VE GONE TOO FAR

The gods of greed and lust and avarice
Finally they've gone too far.
 They took the cup, the Chalice of Life,
 And they've smashed it on the rocks,
 The rocks of hatred toward life.
 We, the people of the Earth,
 We the children of God
 Must fashion a new cup
 A cup of Life
 From which all humanity can drink again
 And be at peace with all Creation
 For that is God's dream
 For all His children.

Grandfather, Great Spirit, I pray
That *Your love within us*
 Will become the guiding light
 By which we your children here on Earth
 Will find our way back
 To the ways of peace and tranquillity and balance,
 For us your children
 And for all your Creation
 Here on the Earth Mother.

We walk about here on earth
Amid great distress and sorrow
 Caused by greed for money
 And lust for power.
 There are those who have far too much
 And those who die because they have too little.
 Have pity on us who have so little courage
 And so little vision,
 Because you gave us all that we need
 To make a better world;
 A world where your dream could be
 The reality of every day, for every one.

It gives me great distress
To see so many pray:

> Oh God, we need this; Oh God, give us that.
> But they seem not to understand
> *That you are already doing your part to the full.*
> But unless we do ours
> Your dream will not be fulfilled
> And the gifts and opportunities you gave us
> Unused.
> Oh God, how we need courage and vision.

The way I see it is that some have never
Been content to marvel and wonder

> At the mysteries of God and His Creation.
> But rather chose to unravel those mysteries
> And "Crack Those Secrets"
> And perhaps one day they would know
> As much as the one who created them.
> That seems to me a deadly situation for us to get into
> Because we do not have the wisdom
> Of the Creator;
> And as long as we live in this human form
> We will be imperfect,
> Because our purpose here is to work toward our perfection.
> What I understand is that the Creation is sacred,
> That it has its own inherent power,
> That it was created in balance and harmony
> And it was to stay that way for all time
> Without interruption.

What I have seen for many years now
Is that there are those children of the Creator

> Who were not content
> With the way that God made things.
> And in their arrogance they set out
> To improve on "His-Her" work;
> They plant trees in straight rows, etc.,
> Everything is done in straight lines
> And right angles
> Yet everything in nature tries to be round,
> It seems like we cannot allow anything
> To be "natural,"

So the tyranny of the right angle dominates our lives
And it seems like there have always been
Those who were obsessed with
"Progress and development."
But I have rarely found anyone who asked:
"Is this progress forward or backwards?"
". . .And this development,
Is it for people or is it for money?"

Have we really progressed when we have
Created weapons so terrible that if they
Were unleashed, this planet would be uninhabitable forever?
Is that the nature of our stewardship?
Have we become so arrogant and so godless
That we can take the gifts of God
And use them to destroy this part of His-Her
Creation forever?
Surely we are laughing in the face of God,
And just as surely we won't do it for very long
Regardless of how it is rationalized.

There were other empires before this one
But they are not here any more
Because each of them came to their highest point
of arrogance
And were each consigned
To oblivion.

Surely it is time to stop and decide
Whether we what to live by the laws
Of God, which are the laws of the universe,
Or continue on our present course
Into oblivion;
We can make a choice.

I believe that those who destroy God's Creation
Will be destroyed by it
Because the Creation has not lost its power,
In spite of how we have desecrated this planet.
And for me the history of "progress and development"
Has been at the cost of planetary and human Life;
Surely the time has come to ask the question:
Why are we here in this part of God's Creation

And what is the purpose of life for each human being?
Are we powerless? Or is the power of God within us?
I say that we have the power of God within us
And the name of that power is L.O.V.E.,
But unless we use it, we too will be consigned
To oblivion.

There is a sacred teaching that says
Thou shalt love thy neighbour as thyself;
      But it's not something to talk about,
      It is a principle to live by or it's not real.

There are those who seem to be infected
By what has been called
      "Nuclear numbness,"
      And there are those who say "I am much too small;
      I can't change anything."
      And there are those who prefer to wring
      Their hands and cry in their beer;
      I would suggest that they have already
      Consigned themselves to oblivion
      Because they refuse to become involved with God's work.
      For me there are only two realities, the negative
      And the positive.
      One is the great negative power, the Destroyer;
      The other great power is the Creator,
      And *we have no choice but to be involved with*
      One or the other.
      There is no middle ground, none whatever,
      That's why I have always been distressed
      To hear people say: I don't want to get involved.

So what's to be done?
I would like to suggest what's to be done
      By starting this way:
      "Those who make private property of the gifts of God
      Pretend in vain to be innocent,
      For in thus retaining the subsistence of the poor
      They are the murderers of those who die every day
      For the want of it."   (Pope Gregory the Great)

The question of nuclear power or nuclear weapons
Cannot be rationalized, they are real;
        But the uses to which they are put can be.
        I can not deal with the technology or
        The rationalization;
        I can only deal with what for me are the
        Underlying fundamental principles of life.

And my understanding, like my knowledge
And my vision are very limited,
        I'm only a human being after all and concerned
        That life should continue on this planet,
        For that reason I affirm all life.
        I don't believe that life was given for us to endure,
        But to reject any notion whatever, which seems
        To be proposed by some that we should move
        Much closer to the possibility of total annihilation
        And celebrate together in a final orgy of death;
        After all, I'm only seventy-one years old and I'm much
        Too young and good looking to die yet.

I refuse to trust my future and my well being
To the military or to governments.
        I do not believe that the way to
        Create peace on earth is to kill other children of God
        Because they are different from us,
        I think there is a better way
        And I think we had better soon find it and use it
        Or forget it forever.

Either we destroy the environment
till it can't support life or,
        We face the possibility of a nuclear holocaust.
        We have a choice.
        We can race on toward extinction
        Or we can choose to live by the laws of the Creation
        We have to choose a course and steer by it.

I have an abiding faith in God, that He will not allow
His Creation to be destroyed by the hands of fools.
        There will be an intervention, and we are close to that time.
        Years ago, a friend of mine blasted me right out of the water,
        He said, "You can't change the world all by yourself,"

But the truth is, I was already changing the world
Because *I was already changing me.*

We either affirm all life or we negate all life.
The choice is ours,
>The free will that is one of our many gifts
>From the Creator is so sacred that
>Not even He will walk around in there,
>Our free will is our responsibility alone
>But we will be required to give an accounting
>For the time, and the opportunities, and the gifts
>That were given to each one of us.

Here I must share a teaching that was
Given to me some years ago by two women.
>I was in South Dakota at an International Indian
>Treaty Conference for four days.
>These two women came to my camp
>They said, "We are Pottawatomi women from Oklahoma,
>And we have no money, and no food, and no shelter"
>So I said, "The young women are preparing food for us,
>And we will share that with you,
>And my tent is up
>And my bed is made,
>So you can have that for yourselves,
>I will find some other place to sleep."
>After we finished eating they came with me
>To where I was working on the skin of an antelope
>That had been killed in the night
>As I worked on the antelope skin
>They told me this story.

They said, "You know, if only people understood
That we, (meaning us people) are spirit beings,
>We have come from the spirit world,
>We have taken on this human form
>But we are only here for a short time
>And we must return again to the spirit world
>From where we have come."

And they said, "While we are here in this human form
        We are the guests of the One who owns all this Creation."
They said,
            "We look around and we see the grass
            And the stones, and the water, the clouds, the trees,
            The fish, the birds and the animals;
            Even the air that we breathe is not ours.
            Surely if people understood that all these things
            Belong to God, surely as His guests, they would not
            Want to destroy these sacred things."
            After they said these things to me they left
            And I never did see them again,
            And I wondered if they might have been
            Spirits in human form,
            But it was a good teaching for me.

There was a Mohawk woman who once said
To the president of the United States:
            "When you have eaten the last fish,
            When you have cut down the last tree,
            And when you have poisoned the last river,
            It's then that you will understand
            That you cannot eat all the gold
            That you have stored away in the bank."

What I have to say about nuclear power
Is that it was all right in the ground where it was
            The way that God put it,
            It didn't threaten anyone, and now that it has been
            Taken out, it threatens all life,
            Surely that is not "progress and development"
            By God's terms.

They have taken from the Storehouse of God's Treasures
The power of the universe, but have not the wisdom
        or the knowledge
        of how to use it.
            I cannot deal with the technologies and the uses
            Of nuclear power; I can only deal with Life
            As I understand it,
            Life, all life to me is sacred,
            Life is not here on this earth *by chance* or *by accident*,

We are given life for a purpose,
And our purpose as I understand it is to live
In peace and harmony and tranquillity,
To accomplish each our own individual destiny
And return to the spirit world from where we came
And our stewardship is to accept our responsibility
To leave this world, this earth, in such a way
That it will be a good place, a happy place,
For other human beings to come to
Knowing that nothing here, not even our own lives
Belongs to us, because there's not one of us
Who can say, "Tomorrow I'll be here."

I would like to share a perception that I have
Which for me is an abiding hope for the time ahead;
I'll describe it this way,
I have to call it *a spirit wind*, it is all pervasive,
All inclusive, it is gentle, and it is gathering strength.
It consists of people whose hearts and minds are engaged
In affirming life, millions of them, all over the earth
Millions more are joining as they see this new direction
For humanity;
This wind, some call it "The Next Wave,"
It is gathering strength and velocity as it goes,
It is made of Love and affirmation
And it will engulf and overwhelm all those
Who are engaged with the negative;
The new day is dawning, what are we waiting for?
Why don't we get up
And celebrate life,
Together

I must continue to lead my people
On the road the Great Spirit made
For us to travel.
We will meet many obstacles along the way.
The peaceful way of life can be accomplished
Only by people with strong courage
And by the purification of all living things.
                    (Dan Katchongva, Hopi Holy Man)

AFFIRMATION

August 5, 1983

Sisters and Brothers
> Of the world community
>> We give thanks to you
>> And we want to celebrate life with you.
>> We, the Native people of this land are your hosts.
>> Let us remember that as children of God
>> We belong to each other.

My perception of God is that He embodies the ecstasy,
> The totality, and the completeness
>> Of the sacred principles of male and female.
>> But I address Him as Grandfather.

My whole purpose for being at this assembly
> Is to affirm life
>> And to deny death, absolutely and completely,
>> We must affirm life for everything
>> That lives on this planet.

My prayer is to God and to you my relations.
> Our final answer to the power of death is *NO*.

And wherever you live on the earth
> Remember that we belong to each other
>> And our purpose is to celebrate life.
>> It is not enough to pray to God for peace on earth,
>> We have to make it happen for ourselves
>> And for each other.

We need to remember
> That it is God's power that we are using
>> And the name of that power is LOVE.

We must go with strong hearts
> And clear minds
>> And know that we cannot fail.

Kitche Manitou, I send this prayer to you.
    I give thanks
        For the power
        And the beauty
        And the sacredness
        Of your Creation.
        I pray for my brothers and sisters;
        I pray that they may learn to use your healing power
        So that we may heal each other
        And learn how to live in peace and harmony
        As you intended.
Grandfather
    I ask you to diminish
        That great evil power.
        Have pity on us
        And help us
        That we may live in peace on earth.

Kitche Magwetch